MARCO

The making of
marco pierre white,
sharpest chef in history

MARCO

Charles Hennessy

Ebury Press
London

First published in Great Britain in 2000

1 3 5 7 9 10 8 6 4 2

Ebury Press
Random House · 20 Vauxhall Bridge Road · London SW1V 2SA

Random House Australia Pty Limited
20 Alfred Street · Milsons Point · Sydney · New South Wales 2061 · Australia

Random House New Zealand Limited
18 Poland Road · Glenfield · Auckland 10 · New Zealand

Random House South Africa (Pty) Limited
Endulini · 5A Jubilee Road · Parktown 2193 · South Africa

The Random House Group Limited Reg. No. 954009

www.randomhouse.co.uk

Papers used by Ebury Press are natural, recyclable products made from wood grown in sustainable forests.

A CIP catalogue record for this book is available from the British Library.

ISBN 0 091 86819 X

Edited by Alison Wormleighton

Designed by Lovelock & Co.

Printed and bound in Great Britain by
Mackays of Chatham plc, Chatham, Kent.

contents

"The professional kitchen is the last refuge of the misfit"
Anthony Bourdain, *New Yorker*

flashes
in the pan

Flash ... In trembling, moonlit bushes in the grounds of Harewood House, West Yorkshire, two small boys crouch, a canvas bag between them. One, sandy-haired, wears a knitted jumper. The other, clearly the leader, sports dark, curly hair, black eyes and a jacket with pockets in which a friendly ferret could feel at home.

They are after rabbits, pheasants, trout perhaps from the lake on the other side of the darkling wood. They are dangerously close in because – as the leader will explain in later years – gamekeepers live on the perimeters of estates, and their lodges, unlike the houses of the toffs, don't have double-glazing to deaden the sound.

At this range, in the golden light beyond the Georgian windows, they can make out the tall, bearded figure of the 7th Earl of Harewood, opera buff but also patron of the local footie club, Leeds United, as he moves regally – his grandad was King George V, no less – among his grand guests. To the crouching boys, to all their mates, he is a remote deity, somewhere between God and Father Christmas. Entranced by the vision, they do not hear the approaching footsteps.

"My gamekeeper nabbed them that time," recalls the Earl. "You don't prosecute a fellow with a bag: a van, yes. They said they were lost, so he gave them 50 pence each for the bus home."

Eschewing the bus and pocketing the cash, the boys return as they have come, across the fields. "I'd rather have had a rabbit," says the leader.

Flash ... The door to the kitchen of a suburban London restaurant with the take-it-or-leave-it name of Harvey's swings violently open and a tall, skinny chef with dark, curly hair and black eyes, in navy and white striped apron ("you have to *earn* your whites"), looks wildly out into the buzzing restaurant. Spying a tall, grey-bearded customer arriving, he flees in a paroxysm of panic back into the clatter of the kitchen. "My God," he thinks, "they've caught up with me at last," as Lord and Lady Harewood, dedicated international gourmets, settle in to check out the work of this new young owner-chef from their home town of Leeds who, everyone has said, is the hottest thing in town.

Flash ... Seated on a leather banquette under the sunny skylights of the recently revamped and reopened Mirabelle restaurant in that most ritzy of London precincts, Mayfair, Lord and Lady Harewood sit and sip the Australian white he has chosen in her honour (she is the sister of the distinguished antipodean hornblower Barry Tuckwell), contemplating the unlikely Provençal garden – pine trees, rosemary, figs, grapes, parasols – among the brick canyons. Unfolding his large frame from another banquette in a far corner of the room, a tall, dark-but-greying-haired figure, fuller now, in tweed jacket from his Savile Row tailor, over – yes – well-earned whites, strolls majestically towards the table and, with a benign smile, greets his friends. "Hello, Marco," says the Earl to the multimillionaire owner-chef. "Thank you for the donation," says his lady, big in charities, to the famously generous ex-poacher. "Enjoy your lunch," he says, and wanders off.

Flash ... Behind the double-glazing of the Georgian windows of Harewood House, among the fine furnishings, the grand guests move about in warm postprandial mood in the golden light shed by the clustered chandeliers. One – tall, dark, curly-haired – detaches himself from the others. He looks out of the window into the darkness, towards the nearby bushes and beyond, to the fields that stretch to another estate. It is the council estate from which he and his chum had so often set off to come here secretly – the council estate where his life, at least for the first six years, had been, as he now acknowledges, "idyllic". After that, though, his paradise lost, "it was a fight for survival".

a birth and a death

In a neat microcosm of the nation, or nations, which Disraeli would have acknowledged with a sardonic nod, the two estates conjoin, nicely encapsulating a society which, uniquely in the world, is divided into two educational, hence social, streams. A boy baby born on the barbered acres of an estate like Harewood (pronounced as spelt, but for Lord and Lady Harewood say "Harwood") would be headed inexorably for prep school, Eton, Oxbridge, before taking up his role in running the country. On the other side of the pale, marked by Nursery Lane, on the Lingfield Council Estate, the scion of the house would be destined just as inexorably for the free education of Fir Tree Primary down the road, followed by Allerton High across the fields, and after that, at 16 – what?

"Have you thought about catering, White?" asked the careers teacher, after the boy had patiently explained why he wanted to be a gamekeeper. (Catering is what they always proposed to pupils they thought thick, the would-be gamekeeper says, and yet the choice would not have been so surprising: his two older brothers, his father and his grandfather had all trained as chefs.)

"You'll never be anything, White," said the master who had beaten him with a plimsoll, in front of the class, for something he had not done. It is not surprising that the tabloids today carry supposed quotes from the ex-victim of injustice – dyslexic to boot – averring that his whole career has been an act of revenge on his teachers.

The same newspapers routinely refer to the icon's origins in "the back streets" of Leeds. But Lingfield was not, and is not, the kind of council estate that the phrase shudderingly evokes in the comfy middle-class consciousness – that contemporary hell of windy walkways, boarded-up doors, urine-scented lifts and discarded syringes. It is a suburban mini-metroland of leafy streets around a sort of village green – useful for kicking a ball about or an evening flirt – composed of neat, unthreatening rows of that quintessentially English phenomenon: the semi-genteel, semi-detached house.

"Nature was part of my life," explains the poacher who would have been gamekeeper. "I'd look out from my council house, and straight across the golf-course was the wood where I could see woodcock, pheasant, partridges, even green woodpeckers. You only had to cross the road, hop over a drystone wall and you were in the fields – it was a magical childhood."

Such souvenirs are not the expected memories of those raised on council estates, but the child born on 11th December 1961 at St James's Hospital, Leeds – healthy, average weight, the third of four boys – and brought back here to live was no ordinary boy (ask his teachers, ask the gamekeepers, ask the greenkeepers). It might reasonably be deduced that the family he was born into, overcrowding the spotless two-bedroom semi at No. 22 Lingfield Mount, was no ordinary family.

His mother, for one thing, was by all accounts something between an angel and a saint, and what's more – the photographic evidence is conclusive – a beauty. She was also Italian, a rare exotic bloom in this bland region where the most exalted flavours were those of Yorkshire pudding and mushy peas and a gastronomic treat was a trip down the road to (the original) Harry Ramsden's fish-and-chip shop. That she – here on a cultural exchange, to perfect her English, and nursing at a local hospital – should have picked out as her life partner a man like Frank White, the very template of a Woodbine-smoking, *News of the World*-reading, greyhounds-going, flat-cap-wearing northerner, provides compelling support for popular theories about the attraction of opposites. (They met at the Griffin Hotel, where he was playing cards between shifts as a chef: it was, she later assured her son, love at first sight.)

Support for the claims to sanctity of the girl born Maria Rosa Gallina at Bardolino on Lake Garda is eagerly supplied by her brother, Gianfranco, now living in retirement in Italy. She was, he says, "a marvellous girl, great-hearted, artistic – she wrote poetry, painted – who would give everything of herself". Her childhood was a happy one, though the war years – her family had moved to Genoa, which as a busy port was much targeted by bombers— brought hardship as well as danger. Their liberal-minded father, Gaetano, a thriving grain exporter, stressed the importance for his children of learning foreign languages (which he taught them himself) and of acquainting themselves with other cultures. Gianfranco had been conscripted into the army, but Maria Rosa, at 24, found herself heading towards England, to London first and then, for reasons that are not clear, to Yorkshire. It was at a register office in Leeds, in 1954, that the sweet-natured, serene Italian girl became the 1st-of-June bride of a man who was in almost every way her cultural and emotional opposite – a man who, one of his oldest friends said, was capable of "starting a fight in an empty room" and who even a loving son says was as "as prickly as a porcupine".

They named their first-born Graham, their second Clive, their fourth Craig Simon. Students of the nuances conveyed by given names within the English social system might see these names, in the context of a northern council estate, as indicators of a certain upwardly mobile aspiration in one or both parents. Whether a recently arrived Italian immigrant would be thus attuned to the subtleties of English social classification is doubtful, but Graham today revealingly recalls that, while his mates' dads would buy them a jacket from Burton's for £20, his father would always go for quality and fork out an additional £50 for something superior from the up-market Dunn's. "We looked different from the other kids on the estate."

It takes no great psychological insight, though, to see in the naming of the third-born – there was a gap of seven years before his arrival – the hand of his mother. Although, according to her brother, there is no record of Marco as a family name, the son so-named has drawn his own conclusions. In the introduction to his mould-breaking first cookbook, *White Heat*,* he observes, "Perhaps with the third son my mother felt she could assert her roots, so she gave me an Italian name." He adds, reinforcing the notion of his status as the chosen one, "For six years I was my mother's child, the youngest, the little boy."

The origins of his second name, Pierre, so useful an asset in his later life as a master of classical French cuisine and so detested in his childhood that he begged his closest mates not to reveal it at school, remain obscure. "I think it was to please an aunt who liked the name," he says with a distinctly Italianate shrug. His mother could hardly have avoided noticing that while her eldest sons were typically sturdy, sandy-haired scions of the north, the baby, with his black, curly hair, was an unmistakably Latinate child. His dark eyes were of an intensity that, as an impressionable lady restaurant critic was later to sigh, "could glaze a crème brûlée from ten yards away".

The view of Maria as the very model of the saintly Madonna is not limited to her family. Gilda Walker, née Porcelli, voluble owner of a thriving pizza restaurant and adjoining shop in Leeds and a pillar of the Italian/Catholic community, remembers her as "a fantastic mother" and "a very, very good cook". Gilda's somewhat more retiring sister, also called Maria, owner with her husband of a flourishing costume company that supplies London's theatres, was especially close. Most mornings, she would call at the modest house on Lingfield Mount, often carrying a bowl of her own genovese pasta sauce, in honour of her friend's birthplace. Together they would wheel their pushchairs, her daughter in one, the infant Marco in the other. She remembers Maria Rosa – for whom she employed the affectionate

* *White Heat*, Mitchell Beazley, 1990.

diminutive Mara – as tall, always smiling, a devoted mother ever anxious to be at home when the older boys returned from school. She also remembers her as – most unusually for one born an Italian Catholic – a religious nonconformist. "You mean, you believe in *God*?" Marco's mother exclaimed one day.

It is little wonder that the then baby of the family, closer for that reason, if no other, to mother than to father, recalls his early years as idyllic. "My mother would walk me to school every morning, collecting me at lunchtime to bring me home to eat with her," he remembers. "Sometimes she wouldn't take me back to school at all in the afternoon because she wanted to play with me. I just wanted to be with her all the time."

Perhaps more significantly for the child's later development, this paradise was not confined to the purlieus of a council estate in grim postwar Leeds, or even to these shores. Every year, extended holidays – the length of the school summer break – were spent with Maria's family in the outskirts of Genoa. (This reversal of the earlier cultural exchange encouraged by his Italian grandfather no doubt helped the boy with his language: "I spoke fluent Italian until I was seven.")

Among the walled gardens, poplars and sun-kissed statuary of Aunt Paola's grand villa on the shores of Lake Garda, or at the house on the hill outside the ancient port of Genoa, the boy would climb cherry trees, fish with his older brothers and swap his catch for

---

* Marco, it might be said, has been poaching fish all his life, although today the poaching is confined to his kitchens and the fishing is the necessary safety valve in a lifestyle that depends upon obsession. That the chosen leisure-time activity may also be obsessive is borne out by the testimony of some of his fishing companions – and of the man himself.

peaches with the local peasants under the watchful eye of Uncle Gianfranco. He remembers his nephew as "a rather plump, small boy" who was "very, very complicated, thoughtful, strong, observant – not like the others. He studied things, and people, a lot."

Writing in *The Times*, Ginny Dougary observed of the mature Marco that "he has turned her [his mother] into a saint, a woman of infinite kindness and grace". Fay Maschler, the respected restaurant critic of the London *Evening Standard*, noted that "he seems comfortable with altering the details [of his early life] from interview to interview, as if anxious to hone the story to its most picaresque".

But Maria's friends the Porcelli sisters had no doubt that she was indeed "a fantastic mother" and "a beautiful lady – but also nice and kind". She was highly respected on the estate, and the headmaster of the boys' primary school was full of admiration for the way she brought up her sons. As for the grown man who had been for six years the baby of the family, his response to Dougary's charge was simply that "I was so young; all I ever saw was good" and "I absolutely adored her". As he is fond of reminding his interlocutors, "The Italians have a saying: 'You may have a thousand fathers, but you only have one mother.'"

It follows that you also have only one mother to lose, and, as another journalist observed, Marco Pierre White's journey to fame and fortune began with the terrible, incomprehensible event that ensured his brutal expulsion from Eden, the loss of a paradise he assumed would last for ever.

• • •

Tragedy, as the poet W H Auden remarked, happens while the banalities of life continue unperturbed: a man walks down the street, somebody puts out a saucer for the cat. It was a normal winter Saturday morning at No. 22 Lingfield Mount. The erstwhile baby of the family, now six, was at home with his adored mother – a situation close to heaven for the boy, for Maria had lately been much preoccupied with the arrival of her fourth son, Craig Simon. "All I cared about was getting my mother's attention again."

The older boys were about their weekend pleasures. Marco remembers seeing the eldest, Graham, running off through the fields in his red T-shirt to go fishing. Marco had begged his parents to go too, but he was housebound, having just returned from hospital with stitches in his knee, the result of a fall. Although it was early February, the day was bright and sunny. He must have looked at the clock, for the time, 9.40, is fixed in his mind for ever, like the smashed watch in a murder mystery. "I often think now that if I had been allowed to go with Graham, I would never have witnessed the scene that has haunted my dreams ever since. But perhaps it was meant to be." Instead he sat in what, on such estates, was always called the lounge, sulking and watching the television, the focus of the room.

Suddenly his mother, tall, beautiful, svelte as always, came out of the kitchen, the baby in her arms. She felt a bit dizzy, she said. Her husband jumped up, took the baby from her and guided her to a chair. Before the baffled eyes of her adoring son, she collapsed into it, unconscious.

"I think I must have become hysterical, because my father sent me up to my room to calm down. I jumped into bed with my clothes on and pulled the covers over my head." The next thing he remembers was being told that the ambulance had arrived. He watched in horrified fascination (his words) as they put his mother on to a stretcher and covered her with a red blanket. "Then I went out into the street and gazed as the ambulance doors were slammed shut on her. I stood watching as it drove away up the hill and out of sight. That was the last time I saw my mother."

The rest of the events of the terrible day were confused. He remembers being sent next door to Mr and Mrs Jackson. Neighbours were people to be counted on in a crisis, and they were very kind to him. His brothers came home and he remembers telling them that "Mum has been taken away". They must, he believes, have understood a lot more about what that might mean than he did –

"but I don't think any of us believed anything really serious could happen to our mother".

In the days that followed, Frank White went to the hospital every evening, returning with sweets for his sons – a present, he explained, from their mother. "I can see now that he must have been desperate to hold the family together and to prevent us from realizing how scared he was himself." What the children did not know was that their mother had suffered a severe brain haemorrhage brought on by childbirth ("cerebral infarction", in the words of the death certificate signed on 20th February 1968). She was alive, but brain-dead, her breathing maintained by a life-support machine.

One week after the collapse of Maria Rosa, Frank White returned from the hospital and, as happens in times of crisis in such families, called the boys into the kitchen. There, he took Marco on to his knee – "he looked awful, as though he were in terrible pain of some kind" – and said, "Your mother has died." It was clearly difficult for him to get the words out, and as he spoke, the reserved, phlegmatic Yorkshireman broke down in tears. "It is the only time I ever saw my father cry."

There are, as the grown man acknowledges, certain things that are impossible for a six-year-old boy to understand. His mother, dead at 38, is one of them. "For weeks, months, years after that, I cried myself to sleep, still waiting for her to come back to me." Still the words that said that his mother was dead meant nothing to him. She couldn't be. He wouldn't let her be.

From that moment, he remembers, he became "a very lonely little boy – and my insecurity has lasted throughout my life". First, though, was the problem of how the death of its most exceptional, most indispensable member would affect the individual lives of the close-knit family – and in particular, that of the one who thereafter had to cope with the matter of "my terrible vulnerability".

nature boy

"You haven't got a mother!" The taunt came, soon after the funeral, from the biggest boy in Marco's class at Fir Tree Primary and it led to an epic fight, outside the school gates, that Peter Crookston in *The Times* was to describe as "White's High Noon". The family at No. 22 had always been different. Now Marco discovered that he had become an outsider: "They all had two parents – I only had one."

The sense of isolation was not confined to school. "I was left alone with two brothers who more or less ignored me. It wasn't their fault, but they had always been close to each other and were at least able to share their grief and give each other support." The baby, Craig Simon, had been sent to Italy to be raised by his uncle, the childless Gianfranco, and to become an Italian boy called Simone and later a policeman and pilot. Like the two older boys, the father – a reserved man, and, as his second boy had observed, "prickly as a porcupine" – never talked about the death. "Being male, I think they regarded it as a sign of weakness to reveal too much emotion," explains Marco. "If only they had realized how much I needed some human emotion shown to me."

At school, at least, Marco could take action. "I knew I had to hide my terrible vulnerability by becoming tough: I had to learn to fight my battles alone." And fight he did, as he here remembers:

He was waiting at the gates, surrounded by a crowd of expectant boys, and my walk towards him was the longest walk of my life, but I knew I had no option; to go back I would be a coward. He pushed me in the face and I fell on the muddy grass. Then he threw me over the bonnet of a car and when I landed I picked up a handful of mud, flung it in his eyes and when he was unable to see, I laid into him, kicking, punching and scratching until he gave in.

Marco's new status as toughest boy in the school – confirmed by his defeats of subsequent challengers – settled more than his current problems. As Peter Crookston puts it, perceptively, "The confidence this gave him, combined with the feeling that he must do something to venerate his mother's memory, had long-reaching effects on his character and made the kitchen of his restaurant [Harvey's] hell for his staff and the dining room heaven for his customers."

Thus Marco (never Pierre) White became a leader of boys, with a following that went on to senior school, and indeed further. Boys from this gang remain today his chosen companions for fishing and shooting weekends and summer holidays. One, the Birmingham-based designer Marcus Steel, head boy at Fir Tree Primary and son of the art teacher (art was the dyslexic Marco's favourite subject), supplies artifacts for his restaurants. According to him, one of Marco's more memorable encounters was with Steel's brother Tim – "a hell of a fight, after which they became firm friends". One of Marco's strengths, Steel feels, is that he remains himself in all circumstances, whereas most of us, from courtesy, or self-interest, or fear, adopt a role or persona we think appropriate to the occasion. "He uses me as a sounding-board in questions of taste, and in the last few years I've learned to be brutally honest with him, which he appreciates."

---

fish tales

Fishing is about freedom and escape. It fills the gaps in my life. Sometimes I'm selfish and I might spend a little long on the river bank. It's as if the little boy has never left me. There's a part of me that's never grown up.

– **Marco Pierre White, quoted in *Hello!***

One instance of this: the two chums from the council estate and primary school are in the Oak Room, the flagship Michelin three-star restaurant in the grand Meridien Hotel in London. Marco proudly shows off his latest acquisition from the auction rooms – a Giacometti table, aesthetically positioned to best advantage between room and kitchen. Steel admires it, hesitates, finally says, "You've got it the wrong way round, Marco." Marco, ever ready for a contestation, replies, "No, I haven't." "Yes, you have." The catalogue is sought, the photo of the *bel objet* found. Steel is right. Without pause, the burly, 6 foot 3 inch chef grabs the table, turns it, positions it to his satisfaction and says, "There!" The 30-year friendship is intact.

Marcus Steel's brother Tim, a slim, alert, articulate, handsome, blue-jeaned, successful TV producer in London, remembers the young Marco – they met on the first day at school, both aged four and a half – as "cock of the school" and a gifted runner but "not 'the boy most likely to succeed'". The young Marco showed no interest in food but was "mad on fishing, shooting and the countryside". For the last five or six years, renewing their friendship in London, they have fished together most weekends. The autodidactic Marco, he says, "takes from others what he wants" in the way of self-improvement. "If he doesn't want to do something, he won't. On the other hand, if he wants to do something, he will – positively."

Steven Briggs – Tim Steel's opposite in articulateness – shy, unworldly, balding, innocent-faced, the kind of man who seems to call out for a big brother's protection – has been Marco's friend for 35 years. He takes a break each summer from selling postcards on the beach at Scarborough to accept a standing invitation to spend, just the two of them, a fortnight fishing Marco's private pond in Hampshire.

Briggs recalls that they spent more time fishing, or collecting golf balls uninvited, or poaching on the Harewood estate, than attending school. (He was helping out in the kitchen at Harvey's on the day that the awesome aristocrat appeared, and once again he hid with Marco, as they had all those years ago.) Briggs has the distinction of having saved Marco's life – as Marco tells it, with typical dramatic spin – by pulling him out of quicksands into which he was sinking on one of their youthful expeditions.

A man who remembers all of these boys with astonishing clarity, is the distinguished director of rugby at Northampton Rugby Football Club ("The Saints"), Ian McGeechan. The ex-Scottish international and coach, ex-British Lions, spent 18 years as a teacher at Fir Tree Primary. In his office, as young giants from all nations surge from the conference room out on to the training ground, the quiet, thoughtful, sensitive-featured man – the antithesis of the beer-punishing rugger brute – who has taken them to the top of the league, reminisces with obvious pleasure about those smaller charges of long ago.

McGeechan, head-hunted from a Leeds high school by the progressive principal, arrived at Fir Tree Primary as head of humanities. For his first two years he taught several subjects to the class of which, so the staff room had thoughtfully warned him, young Marco White was a particularly obstreperous member. In addition, McGeechan took all his classes on cross-country runs through the nearby woods and fields, adding up to four or five outings a day, which helped keep him fit for international rugby duty in those days when the sport was a spare-time activity for amateurs.) The outings also enabled him to discover the talents of the young Marco as a long-distance runner.

More than 20 years on, McGeechan remembers Marco's class with particular affection and precision: "If you were to ask me about any of the other classes in all those years, I wouldn't have a clue." They were not a gang, but a bunch of interesting individuals (the Steel boys, for instance). Although their interests were diverse, there was tremendous cohesion: the group worked well together. Interestingly, he remembers the leader as being not Marco but Tim Steel. They were a creative bunch with whom he liked to sit and talk. How open they were! How adult! "They were outgoing – performers, almost like free spirits: I really enjoyed it." The young Marco was no troublemaker, not even a rebel. At ten, he simply liked to do things his own way. "He was his own person, even then. If you could give him a good reason for doing something, there was no problem; if not, discussion would follow. When he talked about his interests, he was illuminating" (and illuminated: "When he talked about fishing, his face lit up"). Marco was also, McGeechan recalls, physically different. He had long, dark, curly hair, and unlike his mates, who dressed in white shirts or pullovers, he always wore a little tweed jacket.

＊ Translation: "small vines – with tender or sour grapes". The boxed 'vignettes' included here are brief extracts from a few of the almost 100 interviews willingly, even eagerly, granted to the author in the preparation of this book – a statistic surely in itself a testimony to the interest aroused by its subject.

In this small, close-knit society, where the people you saw at school were the people you saw just up the road, out of school, there were few secrets. It was clear that Marco's life was a hard one. He continually made reference to his mother's death. "He missed his mum – she was almost like a goddess to him." But he was also "quite a tough little character – he wanted to win", and a good athlete, "a competitor".

McGeechan also knew about the boy's nocturnal activities: "poaching – I could tell when he had been up all night". About a week – never less – after any excursion that he thought might be of interest, Marco would cheerfully recount the events to his teacher in gripping narrative form. This could be seen as an early example of Marco's later tendency, noted by Fay Maschler, the *Evening Standard* journalist, quoted in the previous chapter, to hone a story into its most picaresque form. It might also be viewed as an early indication of a latent, disciplined creativity which, when fully formed, was to bring fame and fortune to the lonely little long-distance runner.

Fishing and poaching game were only two of young Marco's extra-curricular activities: there was also the exciting, risky but financially rewarding hunt for missing golf balls. There was no shortage of hunting grounds: within a short walk or bike-ride there was an abundance of private greensward – Sand Moor, Allwoodley, Moortown – the club entrances agleam with the more desirable marques of car, the clubhouses baronial.

At certain of these posh enclaves, the young Marco is remembered with unqualified approval. The white-haired, slender, frail octogenarian Ian Duncan, ex-professional at Allwoodley (his father, also a pro, created the Ryder Cup), recalls Marco, who caddied for him, as disciplined, dependable, bright – but also "a loner, anti-establishment", descriptions which Duncan, surprisingly, would also apply to himself. He had had no hesitation in supporting Marco's application – aged 14 – for a gun licence.

Another Marco employer was the Allwoodley all-star Mrs Wyn Walker, surrounded by encased trophies in her mullion-windowed house on the fringes of the course, and sipping tea served by her Filipina maid. Mrs Walker found the boy "so polite" when he came to caddy for her and sometimes for her regular playing partner, the Leeds and England football coach, Don Revie (a Marco hero then and now). She finds him today "a very charming man" who has confided to her that his later success was attributable to the fact that "I wanted to prove to myself that I could do something" and that, his goal achieved, he is no longer ambitious. When he discovered that she had not seen his latest cookery book, he sent her six copies.

A somewhat more complex view of the green-haunting boy is to be heard – in the firm, measured tones of an ex-Coldstream Guards sergeant – in the clubhouse at Sand Moor. Bob Barnes was the greenkeeper of the club, of which his father had been the distinguished professional and course manager. Barnes's usual area of contact with the ten-year-old was as the ardent pursuer of a trespassing urchin, to whom his typical line of address was some variant of "Bugger off, or I'll give you a thick ear!"

His asthmatic, eczema-plagued daughter, who was the unhappy butt of her class at Fir Tree Primary, was championed by her tough but tender-hearted classmate, Marco White. "I know your dad," young Marco told her and she delightedly reported to her father, "He thinks he's bloody Tarzan – but he won't catch me!" The little girl in turn felt sorry for Marco and protective of him for, she explained, he had no mother. "You'd like him, Daddy," she insisted. This was not entirely misguided, for it is the greenkeeper's insight, peering back through the prism of years, that if Marco impinged on his consciousness – "he was very special: I used to see his brothers too, but if you asked me about them today, I couldn't tell you" – it was because he saw so much of himself in the wild lad.

Marco the Nature Boy saw Mr Barnes in all his pomp as the King of the Woods and therefore to be challenged. Bob Barnes saw the lad, with "his little jacket with the ferret in the pocket", as a cunning invader of the territory it was his duty to guard, and therefore a natural enemy, to be caught and punished.

It took some doing, but over-confidence led finally to Marco's downfall. On a freezing winter's day, the greenkeeper saw two small figures on the snow-covered ground, pulling a sled. One was, inevitably, Marco, now 13 or 14 years old. The other was his chum at Allerton High School, Michael Perry (who today, with his wife, designs and manufactures wedding dresses in Leeds and is a frequent visitor, on his sales trips, to Marco's country home). When they spotted the fearsome figure of the enemy, they sensibly turned and ran: Marco, now school champion at cross-country, had long known, to his satisfaction, that he could outpace the burly Barnes. On the brow of the slope, Marco turned to convey a studied, and obscene, gesture of triumph to his old adversary. But the greenkeeper, leaping on to a nearby tractor, cornered the boys, crushed their rickety sled beneath the vehicle and in a measured, parade-ground voice, asked, "Which one of you bastards gave me the V-sign?" Michael Perry prudently remained silent. Marco, brave to the point of recklessness, and also incurably honest, stepped forward and said, "I did." He saw the blow coming, but too late. He remembers the shock to this day. It was a slap heard round the community: the buzz ran along the dusty corridors and through the chalky classrooms of Allerton High – "Bob Barnes has caught Marco!"

In a variant on the many stories told about the unusual

---

fish tales

Last Saturday was one of the greatest days of my life. I achieved my ambition when I caught a 32-pound pike – I have dreamt of that moment since I was a kid. All I ever wanted to do was catch big pike because it is a fish shrouded in mystery, a predator, a monster. There are stories of them eating dogs and ducklings. There are even poems written about them. Because of my pike, I did my Saturday night service on an all-time high – being so happy improves my cooking.

– Marco Pierre White, interviewed in the *Sunday Express*

metamorphosis of the urchin from the council estate, Bob Barnes remembers attending a parents' and pupils' meeting at Allerton High and hearing Marco inform the careers lady that he wished to be "a chef, gamekeeper or pop star". Reminded of this in later years, Marco smiled and said, "Well, one out of three isn't bad, is it?"

Barnes is unhesitant in his praise of his old enemy: "Once you get through that outer shield, there's a wonderful fellow, loyal, protective." (This, understandably, is also his daughter's view.) And some of Marco Pierre White's competitors today, particularly those who have been the losers in the legal skirmishes in which he has so enthusiastically engaged, might be surprised by an old soldier's tribute: "I'd want him beside me in battle. I wouldn't have to watch my back, my sides – they make VCs of people like him."

• • •

If the young Marco's adventures took him far and frequently away from the house in Lingfield Mount, it may be that he felt that, to adapt Oscar Hammerstein's tender lyric in *Show Boat*, "home without her ain't no home to me". Michael Perry never visited his friend but said, "Our house was his home." As the older Marco explained to the journalist Clare Campbell, "My mother's death seemed to divide the family rather than draw us closer together, affecting us all in very different ways. We simply didn't know how to help one another. If only they had realized how much I needed some human warmth shown to me. Instead, I received a father's discipline without a mother's love – an upbringing which left me unstable and with a permanently low opinion of myself." As the normally fearsome interviewer Lynn Barber put it in a rare moment of compassion, "No more cuddles for Marco; the emphasis now was all on being a man."

As a result, he felt, he became "a real teenage rebel" (Bob Barnes, echoing his neighbour the golf pro, called him "anti-establishment"), leader of a pack of schoolboys who admired him for his ability to fight. Thanks, though, to the discipline routinely imposed in this newly all-male household, he and his brothers were always neat and well turned out. Not only did the young Marco, under his father's stern eye, polish his shoes from toe to heel, but he took the longer route along the tarmac paths around the muddy green to school and back, to keep them that way.

If his mother was readily portrayed, in memory at least, as a saint, his father, though no sinner, is not so easily characterized. Frank White, in his son Clive's tactful description, was a "plain-spoken" Yorkshireman of working-class origins (others have preferred the word "abrasive"). He was a trained chef who urged his sons to go into catering – as they all dutifully did, at least for a while – because "people have to eat". His most successful descendant to take up the trade variously describes him as "a bit of a chancer" and a minor businessman who was "into anything that would make money – antiques … anything that would turn £1 into £10". He was a snappy dresser who liked to cut a dash on his frequent visits to the neighbouring racecourses and dog tracks. His son, whose Savile Row tailor visits him for fittings, remembers him "looking like a gangster in one of those great suits with wide lapels and pleated pants, and in long grey overcoats as thick as carpets, and very solid shoes with thick leather soles which made this heavy adult sound as they slap-slapped on the pavement".

Although Marco casually refers to his father as "alcoholic", this is an expression that, as a non-drinker, he employs somewhat liberally, especially about those who have displeased him and make no secret of their love of wine. His older brothers, lager men both, saw their father rather as "a man who liked a drink". What is certain is that, by the time Marco was ten, his father, a heavy smoker, had been diagnosed as suffering from lung cancer. He refused surgery and chemotherapy, on the grounds that he had seen his friends die after both, but accepted painkillers. No doubt, in these circumstances, a glass of whisky was sometimes welcome.

White acknowledges that his father – "an articulate, intelligent man, who couldn't express his emotions" – sacrificed much for his sons, "staying in every night to look after us". (And look after them well: there was never junk food in this house – only fresh, healthy, local produce, simply cooked.) He also taught his sons the Victorian virtues of hard work, urging them to take weekend and holiday jobs washing cars and caddying. It is not clear how much the father ("he couldn't cope with me") knew about his son's idiosyncratic interpretation of his well-meant exhortations. The young Marco, who showed no special interest in food, was busy learning the culinary value of pheasants by selling those he shot at night, using a .22 rifle

---

vignette

It was at The Canteen that Marco decided that he and I would be lifelong friends. Before that, when I was editor of the *News of the World*, I published an interview with him. It was the first time he had talked about his dad, from whom he had been somewhat estranged, and it was the instrument of their rapprochement, so I think he has always felt grateful to me for that. In the working-class milieu of Frank White, the *News of the World* was the only paper that counted [it was a valuable market: in its heyday, circulation stood at more than eight million]. It was only when he read about it in his Sunday favourite that Frank White fully comprehended the scale of his son's achievements. If it was in the *News of the World*, it must be true.

I didn't meet Marco at Harvey's, but I did try to "set him up" there. Rightly or wrongly, he'd gained this reputation for throwing out clients who displeased him. I sent my then assistant editor, together with a woman reporter, to pose as two awkward rustics from the north, who would order the wrong things and generally behave in a way quite inappropriate to the sophistication of the surroundings and occasion. I also booked a second table for a reporter and a photographer, so that when Marco exploded – as of course he was bound to – they would get the story.

When the great chef was informed of the presence of a couple

---

loudly demanding fish and chips, with ketchup, he went straight to their table. Listening to their concocted story of a honeymoon trip, told in convincingly bucolic accents, Marco was deeply moved. "I will cook your fish and chips myself – the best fish and chips you ever ate!" he exclaimed, and returned to the kitchen. When the dish was served, he brought the ketchup himself, and stayed to talk to the odd couple who had so endeared themselves to him. He refused to let them pay the bill. The attempted entrapment may have been a total failure, but at least our expenses had been halved.

He's a hugely complex man, and a serial litigant. He's like a Mafia don. He has a very sharp mind and pays great attention to detail: he wants everything to be right. He will be one of the greats of his generation – one of the most extraordinary people I know. He inspires terrific loyalty: people who have been with him for years love him. Mati changed him. She is brilliant with him, tolerant, lets him be Marco – a creative genius. As for the future, I'm not sure what he should be, but he's getting there! I booked a table for a Valentine's Day dinner with my wife. When we sat down, the waiter served us champagne: compliments of Mr White. Then Marco came out of the kitchen, chatted with us, called for a bottle of wine costing £300, said, 'Don't order, *I'm* going to cook your dinner' and went off to the kitchen. There was no bill. Another time, Michael Winner invited us to dinner. There were four of us and Michael ordered wine at £400 a bottle. The bill came to £1,050 and Michael paid it. Two days later, we got a photocopy of the bill, written on it, "Hope you enjoyed the dinner – Michael." I've had it framed and it hangs in my house.

As a new young editor of the *Mirror*, I committed some perceived journalistic solecism and was publicly reproved by Rupert Murdoch. I got home late, very depressed. There was a call from Marco: "Don't worry," he said, "it'll all sort itself out." It cheered me up enormously.

– Piers Morgan, editor, the *Mirror*

and high-powered torch, and of fish by raiding a neighbourhood trout farm and selling his catch to a local fishmonger.

At 16, then, life, at least superficially, was not without its compensations for the young boy. Although he was small for his age – 5 foot 7 inches, 7½ stone: "I was 18 before I finally shot up" – he more than held his own in fights, won cross-country races, played for the school at rugby and soccer, and ran the fields with his ferrets and his lurcher. But 16 is also the age, unless there is money in the family or higher education in view – and for Marco and all his closest friends, that was clearly not the case – when a youngster must look to his future and the job market. Besides, there were changes at home not entirely to this sensitive youngster's taste.

"When my father remarried, I could not forgive him. If my parents had divorced, it would have been completely different. But as it was, I knew they had loved one another deeply. To me it seemed he was making a mockery of their feelings for one another by marrying again." To others, the arrival of Hazel White in the house went a good way to restoring an air of normal domesticity, and was certainly a comfort to the overburdened, and ailing, Frank. But for the young Marco, who even today insists that "there is a part of me that will remain six years old for ever", the situation was intolerable. "I was certainly not going to accept a substitute, even if he was. His remarriage caused a rift that lasted many years."

It was, clearly, time to leave home.

he's leaving home

In a nice domestic irony, it was the spurned, remarried – "without asking us!" – father who steered the young Marco towards his future, even if the move meant that the dire fate projected by the careers teacher was suddenly to become reality. This was, after all, and in spite of the boy's predilection for country matters, a family with an established catering tradition. Big brothers Clive and Graham, though later rejecting the calling, were both graduates of catering college. His father, like his father before him, was a practising chef who, when he went on a Sunday to help out in his best man's (and best friend's) pub kitchen, would take Marco along as his assistant.

"Go and knock on all the kitchen doors of all the hotels in Harrogate," Dad advised, "until one of them takes you in." It was a shrewd choice of location, for it could be claimed that the main industry of the ancient Yorkshire town was hostelry. (It was in one of Harrogate's hotels that Agatha Christie staged her greatest mystery: her own disappearance.) Although a mere 15 miles north of Leeds, Harrogate was, and is, a world apart, to which people who had the money and the time for such self-pampering came, as the phrase was, to take the waters (they still do, but as day-trippers). Flowers abounded. Among the relics of the spa town's former gentility, alongside the faded grandeur of the cosseting hotels, stood rows of smart boutiques – many of them branches, as in the best resorts, of the capital's finest. They were in sharp contrast to the brief and functional parade, with the fish-and-chip shop as its centrepiece, that formed the commercial heart of Lingfield Council Estate.

As it happened, the first kitchen door that Marco knocked on – acting on his father's urging, for want of any better idea of his own – was that of the Hotel St George, one of the town's four finest, and profitably located across from the conference centre. It was also the last he knocked on, for he was offered a job as trainee chef. At 16, Marco would be pocketing his first wage: £16 for a week's work, and, as he was to discover, in a kitchen the days are long and hard.

There is a revealing phrase in the confessional introduction to the mature chef's first book, *White Heat* (a sort of *livre noir* among cookbooks). "It has taken me a while to admit where I started cooking, but it was the Hotel St George in Harrogate. I was 16 and I didn't want to be a chef. I simply wanted freedom and a good time." For the young trainee, though, there was little opportunity for such psychological analysis:

> I began one day at 7.30am and I can't remember when I finished.
> My first job was to sieve an enormous stockpot. I was given a
> chinois and a small ladle. The stock was a thick, glutinous jelly and
> it took me three hours to force it through the sieve – no one had
> told me to warm it first and then pour it through. They just left me
> to it. No one mentioned eating, either. At 8.00 that night they told
> me to clean a big walk-in fridge and put everything in fresh
> containers. I was absolutely starving and took a fingerful of
> something out of one of the basins. In seconds it was all gone.
> About an hour later a panicking pastry-cook raced through the
> kitchen shouting for the bavarois. I hadn't a clue what a bavarois
> was. It was only when I found out what it was, maybe a year later,
> that I realized I'd eaten what he'd been looking for.

Things could only get better. The problem of sustenance for the growing lad was solved when the chef – in the euphemistic phrase, a "student of the turf" – heard that Marco's father had good connections with trainers and jockeys. Marco was instantly invited to have his meals at the chef's table. Soon the new boy began to feel that he was a real grown-up, staying up till 5.00 in the morning playing poker with the chef and the other kitchen staff, betting £100 on one cut of the cards. An extra-curricular task was added to his duties: "My main job there was bookie's runner for the head chef. I learned a lot about gambling." He also began to demonstrate that capacity for improvisation which was a vital ingredient of his creative talent. Faced with the problem of producing scrambled eggs at speed for up to 150 hungry breakfasters, he found a new use for the steamer gadget that froths the milk for cappuccino on the espresso machine. How were the resulting eggs? "Like rubber."

For the first few weeks of his employment, Michael Truelove – a pal from Leeds some four years his senior who was already working at the St George and is today general manager of the luxurious Crabwell

---

vignette

Marco's a wonderful businessman. Machiavellian to a degree. Only one person in London is more Machiavellian – me! But everything about him is up-front: even his Machiavellianism is up-front! He's a wonderful talker – highly intelligent. His friends leave, but they come back – often with more than one motive. At the moment, Claudio [Pulze] is his *bête noir* – his devil. They change – he has a Devil of the Month! I'm glad he's around. Life would be considerably duller if he weren't. He makes me laugh. You can have a conversation about anything with him, on any level. When he wants something, he can charm anybody: three-star Michelin charm. If he loses that third star, the press will fall on him like wolves. Every time I see him sitting in the Mirabelle [instead of being at the stove in the Oak Room], I get worried. He's very lucky to have found Mati: not many people could manage him.

– Michael Winner, film director, hotel and restaurant reviewer, the *Sunday Times*

Manor Hotel near Chester – picked him up at Lingfield Mount and drove him to and from work. When the manager left, a room became available and was allotted to Marco; he had finally left home, for ever.

"He's got a picture of his mum on the wall," said the maintenance man. "I think the lad's lonesome." He was talking to Frieda Stockdale, who concerned herself with such matters, for in addition to her duties as financial director of the hotel, she was responsible for the well-being of the staff. Those who work in the restaurant and hotel trades are set apart by the nature of their calling: for one thing, our leisure time is their working time. Living in intense proximity with one another, having only themselves as company after the day's or the week's work, they form friendships, go out together, become a family. Frieda Stockdale saw her role as that of formalizing such relationships by organizing outings – often abroad – and other treats. The loneliness of the young long-distance runner was, therefore, even if her motherly instincts had not so directed her, a concern of hers.

The boy was, she found, certainly lonely; he was also shy, but with a barely concealed mischievousness. She remembers his curly, almost black hair and meltingly dark eyes and that he was, in his nice sweaters and tweed jacket, always clean and tidy. After lunch, the two of them would walk the town, do the shops and watch others at their work in the flower market and elsewhere. On Sunday, the day off, Marco would go to Frieda's house and cook lunch (very well too, she remembers, though she recalls an extravagant, almost abandoned, use of pan and vessel, left for her to wash).

Marco had established an immediate rapport with Mr Stockdale: "My husband loved him." Their common interests were shooting and fishing – especially fishing, which must be seen as the second leitmotif, along with cooking, of the future chef's life, in childhood as in manhood. "I am either working or fishing." Already, at 16, he had been winner – for two years running and almost a third – of the junior prize for ocean fishing at the annual Bridlington Festival. (The handsome shield is today on permanent exhibition at his Hampshire home, itself a carefully chosen fishing base.) His friend and fellow competitor on these trips was Lance Shaw, today owner of a thriving packaging-machinery business in Nottinghamshire and still, it almost goes without saying, a friend and frequent visitor.

Shaw recalls, "Luck has a lot to do with it, no doubt, but when everybody's fishing from the same boat, in the same spot, with the same equipment, for the same fish, there must be a reason why one competitor is almost a triple winner. In Marco's case, it was his exceptional capacity for concentration that made the difference. He is totally focused. He never gives up." (Marco recounts that during one of these trips a man died from a heart attack and the competition was naturally halted. "And I was doing rather well," he recalls, with a rueful shake of the head.)

Frieda was also protective of the new apprentice as he learned his trade. In the *batterie de cuisine* of the kitchen at the St George, pride of place went to the imposing metal mincer. It was thus unfortunate that the new boy, impatient with its slow working, wrecked the machinery by thrusting a wooden spoon into its maw. The managing director had no hesitation: the culprit must pay for the damage. To his dismay, Marco's meagre earnings were to be docked by £45. Frieda, fortunately, as head of accounting, was able to "lose" the sum and Marco was saved, which was as well, for here he was taking the first step on a very steep ladder. (It was not the last time Marco was to depend on Frieda's expertise. When he was struggling with the administrative problems – holiday pay and such arcane matters – of his first London restaurant, Harvey's, phone calls to his old protector were frantic and frequent.)

As the writer Lynn Barber observed in the *Observer*, leaving home had "catapulted him out of the working-class world – Harrogate seemed the height of sophistication after his council estate – and also gave him his first taste of responsibilities". The hotel was understaffed. Two of the beginner's first jobs were the preparation of 130 breakfasts (of the traditional English kind: cooked, and served piping hot) and the arranging of the lunchtime buffet. "It taught me how to be organized, how to be quick. And I achieved a certain level of importance, which I'd never been given. My father had always suppressed me; nothing I did was ever good enough. And suddenly I had attention."

After a year of intense apprenticeship, as confidence grew, so did ambition. Versions differ about the moment of revelation. Frieda Stockdale attributes it to a glimpse of the trade journal *Caterer*, being perused by the head porter, who kindly explained to the lad how one could apply for the jobs advertised therein. According to Marco – always to be depended on for the most polished and dramatic presentation of a story, as of a dish – it was all down to a copy of the *Egon Ronay Guide*, an exotic (to the lad from the Lingfield Council Estate) publication picked up in a rare idle moment in the hotel lobby. It had on its cover, he fondly remembers, a picture of a yellow Rolls-Royce parked in front of the Albert Hall in distant London. Buried inside, though, was the real treasure: a rave review of a remarkable restaurant, situated, miracle of miracles, just a few miles down the road from Harrogate, in the small rural town of Ilkley. "Why am I wasting my time here?" he asked himself. "If I'm going to work in a kitchen, it might as well be a good one."

His paradise might have been lost, but he was about to stumble into an Aladdin's Cave.

• • •

To the blasé eye of a metropolitan restaurant critic, writing in *The Times* some years after the restaurant's heyday, "The highly reputed Box Tree … has a whimsical Hansel and Gretel exterior on the main drag, which prepares one for an over-stuffed bar with red flock walls, a twanging guitarist and a collection of paintings that looked as if they had been bought by the lot off the railings of Hyde Park on a particularly poor Sunday … Two blackamoors stoically bearing lamps with umbrella shades guarded the entrance to the restaurant, whose décor developed the main themes of the bar. Could the kitchen be kitschy too?"

To a wide-eyed 17-year-old, though, arriving from the staid surroundings of a provincial hotel, the homely odour of a hundred frying eggs, bacon and sausages and the tasteful decorative touch of two pallid halves of tomato, here was a treasure trove of exotica, a cornucopia of pleasures both aesthetic and sensual – and all in the wilds of West Yorkshire. He was transfixed.

The boy was "overwhelmed by the beauty of the restaurant," Lynn Barber reported in the *Independent on Sunday*, "'like an Aladdin's Cave,' he remembers – the silver, the napery and a French chef in his white clogs bringing an exquisitely coloured terrine on a silver salver. This was his first inkling of what a good 'house' [restaurant] looked like, and it was the birth of his ambition to be a great chef."

The discovery of a calling – in this context, a *métier* – especially when one is young, is a rare and awesome thing, but this was indisputably the adolescent's apotheosis. "His obsession for cooking and his realisation that it was to become his vocation really began … at the Box Tree restaurant, under the tutelage of Michael Lawson," Peter Crookston noted in *The Times*. "Here, even the fabric of the batterie de cuisine delighted him and he would stay behind when everyone had left, lovingly polishing the copper pans."

The mature Marco employs a similar vocabulary. "It was here that food began to become an obsession. Michael Lawson was a gentleman's cook. He'd never had a classical training but had dined in all the two- and three-star Michelin restaurants in France and gained his knowledge that way. His food was grand and extravagant: noisettes of lamb topped with foie gras served with a truffle sauce; roast duck served with three liqueurs. The Mousseline of Sole Réputation sat like a massive cushion on a julienne of vegetables and truffles: it was classic and superb. Michael really opened the door to cooking for me. I still remember with pride the time I made a sauce and he told me it tasted as good as his. I felt secure in my new-found obsession, and lucky to be a part of the Box Tree … I relished every ritual."

His friend, neighbour and regular fishing companion, the novelist Luke Jennings, whose thoughtful profile of the star chef appeared in the *New Yorker*, acknowledges the role of Lawson in the neophyte's development: "… his ambitions awakened, White determined to excel at the *métier* that had been so casually proposed to him." He points out, though, that it was the restaurant's owners who gave the establishment its special aura, its cachet. "The proprietors were Colin Long and Malcolm Reid, known as 'the boys', whom White remembers as 'very camp and very funny'. I'd be whisking eggs, and I'd hear one of them say, 'Ooh, Marco, that's a lovely wrist action. Why don't you come into the larder and earn yourself some cigarettes?' At the Box Tree, White learned the basic elements of classic cuisine, and the importance of restrained luxuriousness."

Whoever should be credited with the achievement, it was a remarkable one: this remote restaurant was awarded two of the coveted Michelin stars at a time when no London restaurant could boast more than one, and Michael Lawson – like Marco, Leeds-born – was the first Englishman to be so honoured. "They would discover one route to a flavour or to a dish," Marco noted, "and would perfect it, etch it in stone. This consistency was a major part of their success, but it was founded on skills that were more domestic in essence than professional."

The traffic, of course, was not all one way. "There was a spark there, I saw from the day he walked in, with his shock of hair. He was very independent but he loved what he saw." So speaks Ken Lamb, ex-baker/pastry-cook at the Box Tree, today in cosy retirement in a leafy suburb of Harrogate. ("You must have one of my cakes: whipped cream has to be eaten within two hours – it won't keep in the fridge.")

Marco, he recalls, had the rare ability to watch someone perform a task he had never seen done before and immediately perform it faultlessly himself. (That gift for concentration, noted by his fishing rival and friend, no doubt helped.) Not only that: he was inventive. The strawberry timbale – a sort of sweet biscuit – was a house speciality, but laborious to prepare: a great disadvantage in a busy 90-seat restaurant. Unbidden, the new lad discovered, by experiment, that by draping the dough over jam jars – as many as six at a time – the job could be speeded up. The Marco White mass-production method is still in use at the Box Tree.

He also began to create his own specialities, using, like his mentor Michael Lawson, not book knowledge (although studying books by, or about, the likes of the master-chefs Escoffier and Point had become, after fishing, his favourite pastime) but the faculties of touch, smell and that developed visual sense which is often the compensatory gift of dyslexics. After weeks of urging by Ken Lamb, the first recipes of Marco Pierre White – the only accredited one, interestingly, is signed "Marco Gallina", the surname being his mother's maiden name – were finally committed to paper at the Box Tree. (A curiosity of the collection is the handwriting: neat, carefully formed - not that of a reputed dyslexic.)

The boy may have been very kind and very charming, as Ken Lamb insists he was, but these qualities did not always keep him out of trouble with his superiors. Called to account for some

---

vignette

I met him at Harvey's, with a colleague. We were there doing a job. We didn't see the side of Marco that everyone else said they saw. Then I got to know him better – and I never saw that side of Marco! There's no doubting his charisma, though. He has a head for business, and he's a winner. He earned one star, then two stars at Harvey's, and kept the two stars when he opened at the Hyde Park. When recognition is given, it spurs to effort. It was an encouragement to realize his potential. I said to him once, "Never forget what it is that made you." Now he is totally dependent on the people who work for him – the aspiring youngsters. They must do it efficiently and consistently. It's a strange relationship: people want to be able to go to a restaurant and say, "He *knows* me" – yet the customer is paying!

– Derek Brown, head inspector, *Michelin Guide*

---

indiscipline or other, Marco found himself sitting across the desk from Mr Reid. No doubt that spirit of independence was manifesting itself in the commis-chef's comportment. "When I'm talking to you, young man, you look at me," Mr Reid shouted. Ever polite, Marco raised those liquid orbs, bestowing upon his boss that wonted gaze of transparent, fearless honesty. "Don't you look at me like that!" Mr Reid cried.

The boy could hardly be criticized for idleness. His colleagues of that time are as one: "A very hard worker," says Michael Truelove, who, at Marco's instigation, had followed him from the St George. Simon Gueller, chef-proprietor of the one-star Rascasse in Leeds, goes further. "Nobody could keep up with him. He was driven. Even when he had been up all night, he always worked tremendously hard." Gueller, four years his junior, was very close to Marco. Neither had many friends. "He was very generous, very good to me – more like a brother than my brother." He is also, Gueller says, "incredibly honest – which can be disconcerting to some. If I have a problem, he is the first person I would call; and if he had a problem, I would drop everything to help him." Will his startling success continue? "Marco is too clever to undertake something at which he is not going to be successful."

Further success, after two years at the Box Tree, would require a move, and almost certainly, a move south. The Yorkshire restaurant had given him, at one remove, so to speak, an introduction to the mysteries of French classical cuisine – but the talk in the trade was that a pair of distinguished chefs (one of them cook to the Rothschilds, no less) had arrived in London from France itself, and were spreading the true gospel.

To get an interview with the celebrated Roux brothers, however, the lad would need a reference, and his relationship with "the boys" was not such as to guarantee that one would be forthcoming. He appealed to Ken Lamb for help. Lamb had – no doubt squirrelled away with the precious recipes – a couple of sheets of Box Tree headed notepaper. In the guise of head waiter (which was not too far from the truth, as he had been first engaged as a waiter) he composed the following prescient recommendation:

> Having known Marco since he was 16/17 when he worked here at the Box Tree restaurant, and recognising even at that early age the intense feeling and strong natural ability in the production of innovative "haute cuisine", I was delighted to hear that a two-star Michelin chef recently said to the Box Tree staff dining with him, "Some day you will be proud you knew him!"
>
> I am quite sure that the developing skills of this young man will become even more well known in the future and I wish him well and recommend his ability to whoever it may be of concern.
>
> (signed) K Lamb
> Head Waiter, Box Tree

Armed with this glowing testimonial, the young man set off towards the unknown south.

capital ideas

"Maybe I had to come south because I was so different to the people around me." London, a more detached observer suggested, was perhaps Marco Pierre White's Paris (a place he has visited once, for all of four hours, most of them spent in a kitchen at the Longchamps racecourse). In the unlikely purlieus of Ilkley, he had worshipped at the altar of French *haute cuisine*, but the services had been conducted by mere acolytes. In London he would find the high priests of the calling: the contemporary equals of those masters – Pellaprat, Point, Dumaine, Escoffier and the rest – whose works he had pored over in the brief hours away from the torrid temple.

The arrival on these shores from Paris of the Roux brothers – Albert, the older and stouter, and Michel, the taller and thinner (physically, at least, a proven combination for success in a double act) – changed the face of British gastronomy, such as it was, dramatically and for ever. The creation of a temple of the art in an un-chic corner of Chelsea (as one of its denizens might put it, not Sloane Street but *Lower* Sloane Street, my dear) gave London its first bastion in that chain of strongholds that represent the acknowledged summit of culinary skills: the Michelin three-starred restaurants.

The red *Michelin Guide to Hotels and Restaurants*, reverently hailed by one writer in the field as "the greatest work of collective authorship since the King James version of the Bible", is the only arbiter of their skills unquestioningly accepted by all ambitious chefs. Awards by such as Gault & Millau or Egon Ronay, though welcome, are as gravy to the main course. The selection of great Michelin three-star restaurants, fewer than 20 in all, had – with the exception of the odd outpost in francophone Belgium and Switzerland – been rigorously, some would say chauvinistically, confined to France. The Michelin definition of a three-star table (the award is purely for the quality of the cooking and its service in elegant surroundings) has remained unchanged almost from the guide's beginnings: "exceptional cuisine, worth a special journey", with the rider that "one always eats here extremely well, sometimes superbly".

Whether the Roux brothers would have achieved the peak that they successfully scaled in London had they remained in Paris is open to question. In fact, the British connection was established early. Michel, the thin, elegant, actorly one, had trained as a *pâtissier* with the house of Loyal. His first job as chef was at the British Embassy; from there he moved a few doors down the Faubourg-St-Honoré and into the employ of the legendary hostess Cécile de Rothschild, with whom, given an unlimited budget and *carte blanche* for the *carte*, he was happy to stay for six years.

His big brother, meanwhile, had established himself in the heart of England, as chef to the Cazalet family, who trained the Queen Mother's horses. The brothers, thus comfortably ensconced in embassy, town house or country mansion, had hitherto avoided the cut and thrust of the commercial market. But they were trained professionals and, more importantly perhaps, came from a family with a highly developed culinary awareness (they used some of their mother's recipes in their restaurant, Le Gavroche). Moreover, they had been raised, as no English chef could have been, in an endemic restaurant culture.

In France – as in Italy – culinary development has been organic: restaurants arose from the soil (which provided the basic materials in abundance), by way of the private home, the small bistro and the family-run *auberge*, on to the renowned shrines and temples. Leave a three-star restaurant in the provinces of France and within a few hours' drive, passing many a beguiling one- or two-star establishment, you will find another. In England – as in America – the few outstanding restaurants have been parachuted, so to speak, on to a gastronomic desert. Leave Michel Roux's three-star restaurant at Bray and you may drive the length and breadth of the countryside, passing a thousand uninviting fast-food cafés, and never find another three-star establishment. (Even in the capital there are a mere two.)

The cuisine in France (like the education system) is democratic: everybody eats the same food, at more or less elevated levels of sophistication. In England, as in most other aspects of social life, there are two nations, the one catered to by the Little Chefs, the pizza joints and the "ethnic" establishments, the other by the (few) outstanding chefs.

There being no native cuisine (well, what is it?), it is hardly surprising that what the top British chefs offer their customers is, unashamedly, French classical cuisine. It is not surprising either that when not one but two native practitioners of that art – Michel having decided to join his brother – announced their arrival in the capital, the ambitious young chef from Yorkshire was hot on their trail.

Marco's road to the dreamed-of portals was somewhat circuitous, however: the most direct route from Leeds to London does not lie through Hampshire. In fact, he had written to the Roux brothers' renowned Le Gavroche in search of employment, only to discover that the application form was in French. There being no such problem with the highly reputed Chewton Glen, in New Milton, Hampshire, he applied to that establishment instead. He was granted an interview, and took along the reference his friend Ken Lamb had written. Whether the job interview at Chewton Glen (with the chef,

vignette

We had gone to Harvey's for dinner, and Marco wanted us to have pig's trotters, a speciality, but we had lunched too copiously, and declined. As we were leaving, he arrived with a package: two portions of pig's trotters! Later, at home, a motor-cycle messenger arrived: Marco had forgotten the sauce!

– Lord and Lady Harewood

Christian Delteil, who had obtained a Michelin star for the establishment) went well or badly is no longer remembered by either party but, in view of what followed, hardly matters. The young candidate, on emerging into the countryside, became confused by the mysterious geography of the unknown south. "I got lost, and by the time I arrived back in London, I'd missed my coach." He remembers that he had only £7.36 on him. "I couldn't afford bed & breakfast, so I walked the streets all night, waiting for the first coach to Pontefract [in Yorkshire, where his father was to meet him] in the morning."

All he retained from his only previous visit to London was a memory of his mother taking him to see the Changing of the Guard at Buckingham Palace. Victoria Coach Station being conveniently close to the royal town house, he set off on a sentimental journey. On the way – Victoria being also adjacent to Chelsea – he found himself outside a restaurant: it was, as it happened, Le Gavroche. He had stumbled on the Holy Grail. "It was all lit up," he recalls, "and I peered through the windows like a street urchin." (An interesting choice of phrase: had his French been good enough to allow him to fill in the application form, he might have realized that *un gavroche* is, in fact, a street urchin.)

White returned the next morning, knocked on the door and was told to go to the Roux head office, across the river in Wandsworth – coincidentally, the scene of his later triumph. The cash-strapped urchin again set off on foot and, on arriving, "there was Albert Roux sitting behind a desk. I gave him the reference I had brought with me for Chewton Glen. He asked where I'd worked and whether I had digs and said, 'Come down on Monday, we'll find somewhere for you to live and you can start on Tuesday.'"

The offer, it seems, was conditional on the wild-eyed applicant's obtaining an immediate haircut. It was an understandable reaction of a distinguished chef to the appearance of the young man with long matted locks who, according to the journalist Lesley Ann Jones, "would look at home frying onions in a hot-dog truck outside Wembley Stadium or shifting amplifiers for pop groups".

But the rapport between the two seems to have been instant and profound, hardly surprising in view of their subsequent assessments of each other. According to White, "Albert was responsible for what I have today. I was inspired by his honesty, his attention to detail." Roux described his protégé as "my boy who does the work of ten men" and declared him to be "the best natural cook" he had ever worked with. "His genius is reflected on the plate."

Of the initial encounter, Roux remembers, among less flattering physical details, that "his eyes were blazing like fire". As he recalled to the journalist Shirley Lowe, "Marco came into my office, looking for work. He was from Yorkshire, a bit rough, tired – but he made an impression. I looked at the shining eyes, I saw a lot of determination and power in them. The stare was hard, you know. I told him to go and get a haircut, which he did, and I gave him a job." To the *New Yorker*'s profile-writer Luke Jennings he explained, "I hired him for his personality. He had those deep, deep eyes, and he was very convincing."

It would be intriguing to see how the young man, Roux's "little genius", who was, according to his mentor, "running at 100 miles an hour", got along in the interminable, hard, hot hours of the kitchen with the older man who, according to his protégé, was "one of the few people who could control me". What is certain is that the mature, Michelin three-star chef of today would readily subscribe to the culinary philosophy expounded then by the equally starred earlier master: "Loving food is a full-time occupation, and the preparation of it is emotionally as well as physically exhausting. You have to adore food to be good at this. You've got to be good at giving to be good at cooking. I don't know any good chef who is mean."

Michel – today owner-chef of the elegant Waterside Inn at Bray – recalls a singularity of Le Gavroche when it opened as a modest, bistro-sized establishment in April 1967.

As chef to the Queen Mother's trainer, my brother often had the
Royal Family as "customers": his dishes were therefore "*des plats de*

maison", and I had my "*plats de maison bourgeoise*" from the Rothschilds. So we devised a menu that brought together the things we knew. There was canard rôti challandais – we had the duck sent especially from the Challans region of the Vendée – loup au fenouil, homard à l'escargot, sauce béarnaise, a pot au feu, sauce Albert and lots of others: the Soufflé Suissesse, for instance. It's a soufflé that's removed from the mould halfway through the cooking, and finished with a topping of cheese – half gruyère, half cheddar – on a base of crème fraîche. There's a dish that is totally unlike your traditional cheese soufflé – and it's still a huge success at Le Gavroche today.

Since, as has been previously noted, *all* classical French cuisine is of demotic origin, the claim to domesticity is confusing. To the newcomer in the kitchen, what was on show was not "domestic" – a word Marco has since applied to the version of French cuisine he had encountered, with such delight, at the Box Tree. That was cooking based on a remembrance of things past: the fruit of the discoveries made during trips to France by the chef and the owners, and recreated, by trial and error, in a Yorkshire kitchen.

Here, though, was indisputably the Real Thing – classical dishes from a centuries-old repertoire, cooked, with style and panache, by two Frenchmen as to the manner born. It was why Marco was here. As a result, according to Albert Roux, "he acquitted himself twice as well as anyone else in the kitchen, but he had to be restrained, told to calm down". The intensity, the concentration that had led to achievement (in fishing as in cooking) here manifested itself in ways that his co-workers could hardly overlook.

"He was always banging saucepans, pushing people," his mentor told the journalist Shirley Rowe. "Not rudely, you understand, but anxious to get on. There was an enthusiasm to prove he was good at what he was doing." The young Marco – still a lowly commis, only one rank up in the brigade from the kitchen porters who washed the dishes – was "inspired by his [Roux's] honesty, his attention to detail. He taught me the proper use of extravagance." Roux had no doubts about the special qualities of the scruffy youth who had stumbled across his threshold:

> He was born to cook. The way he touched things, the way the sauce came out, the way he followed what you said but executed it better than you expected, better sometimes than you could yourself. Marco was a character. He came out from the rest of the pack. I became protective of him because I had taken to him. I have never felt that deep feeling, not with the others who worked for me.

These sentiments are fervently supported by Marc Beaujeu, for 20 years executive chef to the Roux brothers and now, working out of New Covent Garden, supplier of foie gras and such to the classier restaurants, including those of Marco Pierre White:

> I have seen a lot of chefs, commis and the rest in my time, but this guy was different. He was quite amazing. Not only was he a very hard worker, he was a very funny man! When he decorated a plate, he was totally concentrated, obsessive but organized and meticulous; the result was a work of art – you could tell a Marco plate from anybody else's.

Le Gavroche was open for dinner only; that left Marco free to seek additional employment, and extra money, at lunchtime. Another chef, Nico Ladenis, was making his name. Chez Nico was across the

---

vignette

Marco is a free thinker. My boundaries were set by tradition: school, college, family. Here I can do what I want to. What things *look* like is important to Marco. Our food is clean and simple – if it's dressed, it's dressed for a reason. He's a leader. There's no fear in Marco's kitchens. Marco shouts, but he doesn't hit anyone.

– Robert Reid, head chef, Oak Room

river in Battersea, and the young Marco raced daily between the two kitchens – giving his all, of course, in both. Marc Beaujeu recalls this period:

> He was often late, often unshaven, and I would have to give him a good talking-to. When we met recently, he gave me a reproving look: "You used to be very tough with me," he said. I replied, "But look where you are now – you are the master!" When he opened his first restaurant, Harvey's, I went to dinner there. He came to our table and said to my wife, "One day, I will be at the top." Well, he is!

The eccentric comportment of the young man was not confined to the workplace. The writer Lesley Ann Jones recalls a domestic scene at a time when White was still an employee of Roux: "When we went to the country estate of Albert Roux for a fishing weekend and Monsieur Albert lovingly prepared the most exquisite coq au vin for Sunday lunch, served with Chablis from his own vineyard, Marco appeared at the lavishly laid table in a dressing gown and promptly fell asleep."

Although a quarrel – not unusual in the social and business life of the mercurial White – has in recent times clouded the relationship (such clouds invariably pass), the mutual regard of the two men is obvious from their own declarations. "We've become really close friends, but I still call him chef. It's a mark of respect," says White of his former boss. Of his ex-employee, Albert Roux says, "He is not how he has been portrayed (with relish) by the press. The MPW I know has got a very big heart, and certainly behind that big frame is a soft, kind person who understands the reality of life. He's extremely well learned, if not educated. There's a difference. Those brown eyes make use of what they're seeing around him."

One of the things those watchful eyes could hardly have missed was the fact that, as well as introducing to an eager clientele the wonders of *haute cuisine*, the Roux brothers – well before Terence Conran, who anyway was not a chef but a designer/retailer – were creating an "empire". Soon, besides the award-winning Le Gavroche, there was Gavvers, Le Poulbot in the City, the Waterside Inn at Bray, La Boucherie Lamartine (selling directly to the public the meat and other products supplied for their kitchens), a company marketing hermetically sealed (*sous vide*) fresh food (and, as outlet for it, a restaurant, Les Trois Plats) and another restaurant, thankfully short-lived, called Rouxl Britannia. The brothers – their double act coming into its own – were also the first serious (as opposed to entertainer) TV chefs, the first to become, as Paul Bocuse had been in France, celebrity chefs, their exploits fodder for the popular press. What use the unknown Marco Pierre White – "a chield's amang you taking notes"* – was to make of this would soon become apparent to a wider world.

* From 'Captain Grose's peregrinations through Scotland' by Robert Burns.

master classes

"I didn't stop still, I didn't have time for sleep or social life or anything else except cooking, learning, working, thinking." For a 19-year-old stranger in the city, it was quite a syllabus. Something, as they say, would have to give.

He was cooking for Nico Ladenis in the mornings, for a weekly £50, and for Albert Roux in the afternoons and evenings: cooking, that is, and learning, working, thinking. This was no mere galley-slaving. Nico, like Albert, was a chef of high ambition, which in culinary terms meant that his goal would naturally be working towards the achievement of a Michelin star, and then another, and then – why not? – a third. (In a poignant dénouement, the only three-star restaurants in London today are those of Nico Ladenis and his young disciple.) In his first book, *White Heat*, the pupil paid tribute to the master:

> He is the true gourmet. I've never met anyone who had as much
> appreciation of food as Nico does. He loves eating. If he hadn't been
> a great chef he would have been the most knowledgeable and
> respected food journalist. But he's also a great technician, and he
> runs one of the most consistent restaurants in the country. I
> suppose I learned about the slow pursuit of perfection from Nico,
> the constant quest to lift everything one notch higher the whole
> time. He's exactly double my age, he's moved his restaurant five

times, and he's still chipping away, refining, never faltering. You
need incredible strength and resolve to do that. For me things
change all the time … everything goes up and down, the world is
all peaks and troughs; Nico's up there on a plateau, checking the
compass to make sure he's on course.

If the older Marco's self-analysis is correct, and if working with Nico
was a peak in his life, what followed could fairly be described as a
trough. Marco left his jobs and went on what, with typical
theatricality, he describes as "a big bender", becoming, as he puts it,
"a gastro-punk". Since the boy from what he equally imaginatively
calls the back streets of Leeds was, and remains, immune to the lures
of drink and drugs and since the bourgeois bohemia of Chelsea hardly
qualifies as a location for a Dostoyevskyan descent into the lower
depths, it may be that the chef has been niggardly with the salt.

Alan Crompton-Batt, doyen of London's gastronomic spin-doctors
(PR consultant for, among others, Marco Pierre White's Mirabelle),
remembers it well: "He was 19. We met regularly at one café or
another and drank too much coffee and smoked too many Marlboros.
He worked when he needed cash, helping out in restaurants where the
cooks were totally ignorant of the things he already knew: he taught
them, for free." At first this existence – which for the young of today
would amount to not much more than hanging out in the King's
Road – came as an agreeable break in the punishing routine of the
kitchens, which had been his world since he left school: "It was great
to be decadent – at first, anyway. But eventually I couldn't stand
watching another person getting drunk or someone else injecting
smack into their veins. Eighteen months and I'd had enough of the
world outside. I needed to get back into the kitchen. But in culinary
terms, I'd cooked my goose."

It was another Frenchman – and another future three-star chef –
who, as Marco later put it, "started me on my rehabilitation course".
Marco's motives for the move may have derived from the need for
survival – although, as he had always done, even in his desperation he

went for the best, for the person who could contribute the most to his development, to his as yet unstated (perhaps because unacknowledged) plan to get to the top.

Pierre Koffmann, "the chef's chef" (the equivalent in stature of the admired Joël Robuchon in France), took an equally equivocal view: "Marco only came to steal my recipes. But he's one of the best chefs I ever had in my kitchen – always looking, always listening, wanting to absorb as much as possible as quickly as possible."

Koffmann's suspicions may have been well founded. In his *New Yorker* profile of his friend, neighbour and fellow-fisherman, Luke Jennings notes:

> These chefs [Roux, Ladenis, Koffmann, Blanc], although none of
> them were British-born, represented the British *haute-cuisine*
> establishment of the early eighties. Like a spy, White submitted
> himself to the discipline of their kitchens, remembered everything
> that he heard and saw, and moved on. His employers, he knew,
> would soon be his rivals, and he was determined to surpass them.

The rehabilitation course at Koffmann's famous restaurant, La Tante Claire, started early one morning, Marco recalled, "when I turned up out of the blue ... and asked if I could work in the kitchen for a day – without pay. I turned up again the next day, and the next, and every day for a month, until finally one of his team left and he was able to

---

vignette

I wouldn't be here if it weren't for him and for that I'm grateful. But he said he was going to do this and he was going to do that and within six months he'd left us. He never actually put his own money into it and then he just disappeared, my other backer pulled out and I had to pick up the pieces.

– Eric Couillère-Chavot, ex-Harvey's, chef-owner Interlude de Chavot, in which Marco had a 50 per cent stake

---

offer me a paid place in the kitchen. I had to prove myself all over again, completely."

Koffmann soon perceived that here was a lad who was prepared to stand outside in the cold, uncomplainingly cleaning scallops. He saw that Marco could deftly perform the tricky feat of scooping out quenelles in one go. Eventually he was included in the chef's teatime, and knew that he had earned the great man's respect.* "It took time, though. Unlike me, Pierre doesn't talk when he works – his is a silent kitchen. He expresses himself in his food. You see Pierre on every plate. He serves what he likes eating, not what will earn him Michelin stars."

Marco learned – he claims – two other lessons from Koffmann. "I learned about bread from Pierre. He has a passion for bread. Serve good bread and butter before the meal and all will be well." The second lesson, which some observers would claim has not yet been totally absorbed, was that of "humility – not my strong point, I know. Pierre has shunned publicity all his life. Perhaps one day I'll be at one with myself, as he is. Who knows?"

The young spy, having come in from the cold, now made for open country. There being, presumably, no more secrets to uncover *chez* Koffmann, after six months he turned, at the age of 23, in the direction of the last of the "establishment" masters: the self-taught Raymond Blanc, in his ambitiously conceived and archly named redoubt, Le Manoir aux Quat' Saisons, in the countryside near Oxford. Before he went, Marco promised Koffmann that he would stay with Blanc for a year. "So I did. I needed the credibility."

What credibility he already possessed underwent a severe testing from the start. According to Stephen Yare, then in the kitchens at Le Manoir and today owner-chef of the Michelin-listed Hedgehogs restaurant near Ipswich, the young Marco chose to arrive at the sedate

---

* It was Koffmann's custom to be served tea, which he drank from a bowl, before lunch and after evening service. He was a man of few words, and his invitation to Marco to join him on these occasions was a welcome sign that he was accepted. This was particularly meaningful to Marco, since he was the only English person on the staff and easily excluded from the inner circle by language and other factors.

manor house for his interview wearing a fetching black cape and jackboots.

"He was charismatic and I knew immediately that he was going far, that he would scale the highest pinnacles. He had great drive, and at work he was a perfectionist: he would take a dish and hone it down to its essentials." He was, though, as Yare delicately puts it, "difficult to harness". Interestingly, White himself makes use of the same imagery: "Raymond couldn't hold the reins on me. I was in a hurry, and too talented for my age. He knew that I had flair – and I knew that I had flair."

Another worker in the kitchen had reason to be grateful for Marco's arrival. Seventeen-year-old Heston Blumenthal, English-born descendant of a Latvian Jewish family, had dreamed of being a chef. Having trained at the Westminster College of Catering, he had been taken on as an apprentice by Raymond Blanc. Compared with his dreams, he found the kitchen – as all kitchens are – hell, and his colleagues brutal. Marco immediately and instinctively assumed the role of protector during Heston's brief stay, and became a friend and guest of his family ("an excellent guest, shy and polite: he always called my father 'Mr Blumenthal'").

Heston escaped to become financial controller in a leasing company until, his earlier vocation reasserting itself, in a pattern that was the reverse of his protector's career, the businessman became a chef. With Marco's help – "he has a heart of gold, and now that he is successful, he doesn't forget his friends" – he opened a small bistro in Bray. The plucky little competitor to Michel Roux's grand Waterside Inn in the same village was called The Fat Duck. (The name was Marco's suggestion: when asked why, he asks, why not?) In 1999 the frightened apprentice won his first Michelin star: some would claim that his potato purée is at least the equal of the great Robuchon's renowned creation.

Although Marco can, as he puts it, "throw something on a plate and it will look wonderful", there was still something of Blanc's that he could study and make his own. "It was with Raymond that I developed my sense of taste. Food should taste of what it is – that's common sense, of course, but few people realize it. Raymond does. He has an extraordinary sense of taste."

Marco was also, as ever, carefully observing the psychological make-up and comportment of the individuals with whom he came in contact. He came to the conclusion that "of all the chefs I worked for, I know I'm most like Raymond. There's an element of madness in us both. It's only a matter of time before the asylum catches up with me or with Raymond. Perhaps they'll get us both in the end. Then we won't be in chef's jackets, we'll be in straitjackets."

Blanc, in turn, had ample opportunity to observe his pupil, and his conclusions, as reported by Fay Maschler, the distinguished restaurant reviewer of the London *Evening Standard*, were mixed. "It would take someone very foolish to say that he wasn't a good cook," Blanc told her, but he added ("reasonably, it seems to me," Maschler decided) that Marco has to embark on a "hell of a lot of consultation with himself before he can sort out the truth from the lies he tells himself and others".

In fairness, it should be borne in mind that Maschler's sympathy for Blanc's views was influenced by her own unhappy experience with his subject. Maschler – who claims to have been the first to applaud the youngster's talent in print – reflected in her column on the more mature chef: "Marco does seem to have mellowed. The chap who a few years ago put it about London that I gave him a critical mention only because he refused to give in to my entreaties to go to bed with him – an annoyingly difficult charge convincingly to refute – now appears nigh on gallant."

Another Londoner, a student at Oxford at the time, has a similarly sexual complaint: "He always took my girlfriends!" Piers Adam, founder of the trendy K-Bars, showed early indications of his *métier* by running a weekly nightclub and organizing college balls – with the help of a moonlighting Marco, whom he had met in the bar of Le Manoir. "We struck it off immediately, and he was always around after that. He is the most talented man I've ever met – an artist, a creator, and with a razor-sharp mind and an extraordinarily magnetic personality." They were both, he notes, starting out at the same time, and "Marco had visions of grandeur: now that he has achieved that, he has mellowed"; then, though, for all his "incredible self-confidence", he was also "a little boy lost", vulnerable, complex. Adam, like so many of Marco's early acquaintances, is a regular customer at his grand establishments (the less affluent are usually there as Marco's guests). "Everybody wants to be adored by him: I am very fortunate Marco came into my life."

For the young apprentice, the year with Blanc, fulfilling his promise to Koffmann, was at an end, and Marco had run out of great French chefs to spy on. (He saw himself as "a closing chapter of the eighties – a finale. The Roux brothers, Pierre, Nico and Raymond: they each have fledglings coming through now. But I'm an offspring of them all, a hybrid.") The solution to the problem was obvious: like many another young English chef before and since, he would return to the source – he would go to Paris.

He packed his bags, telephoned an old friend, Alan Bennett, in London, and asked if he could put him up for a few days while he made his travel arrangements. Bennett – who owned a restaurant, Lampwicks, in that popular eating-site, Queenstown Road, Battersea – told him to pick up the keys to his flat at the ironmonger's opposite. When Marco walked in, he found the flat denuded of furniture: Bennett's wife had left him, taking the children and, it seemed, everything else. The restaurant was not doing well and there was no money to pay decent staff. Instead of heading for the Channel, White, camping in the bare flat, stayed on to help, cooking for his friend, without wages, for five months. Bennett, meanwhile, was negotiating with two of his customers to buy a site in the inner suburb of Wandsworth and open a new restaurant, which, he hoped, would be more successful and solve his pressing financial problems.

Sadly, Lampwicks closed. Marco, needing to replenish his funds, found himself, as at the beginning of his career, knocking on kitchen doors. Again, he was lucky: the first door was that of the long-established Leoni's Quo Vadis in Soho, and it was opened by the owner (of the restaurant and the building), the Lebanese-born Jimmy Lahoud. "When I saw this skinny boy, with long hair, dressed in a studded leather jacket, I didn't get the right impression – but when I saw him working in the kitchen, I realized he was in a different class to anything I'd seen." Lahoud was then 37 and wealthy, Marco 24 and broke. But the older man enjoyed the younger one's company so much that he would take him out to dinner: "And believe me, I do not normally take my chefs out to dinner."

Although the two were later to become (most profitably) business associates, an unexpected telephone call to Marco brought a temporary end to their relationship. One of Bennett's two prospective partners in the Wandsworth deal was Nigel Platts-Martin (today co-owner, with Marco's ex-pupil, the talented chef Philip Howard, of the two-star Square in London's Mayfair). He explained that Bennett – who later committed suicide – was unable to raise the money for his share of the investment and that Marco would be welcome to take his place. If he did so, Platts-Martin, a successful city broker, would arrange a bank loan for him of £35,000.

Thus, in 1987, at the age of 25, Marco was enabled to buy his own shares in the company and become an owner-chef – albeit of an obscure restaurant with the meaningless name of Harvey's, which was, everyone said, too far from the centre of town to attract the carriage trade. Wandsworth was considered, even by the motorized classes who were his potential clientele, a Thames bridge too far to travel to for a meal.

France's loss was to be England's gain.

satanic suburbs

"I was astonished that a humble, small place, run on a shoe-string, beset with operational nightmares, its kitchen staff hardly out of their teens, run without previous managerial experience, should, so soon after opening, attain such a high degree of excellence." Thus Egon Ronay, a man not given to hyperbole, writing in the *Sunday Times* on 8th March 1987, staked his claim to be the first food critic to hail a new star in the culinary firmament. (There is a pre-empting counter-claim by Fay Maschler of the London *Evening Standard*, who, as already mentioned, appears to have spotted the work of the anonymous young wizard in the kitchen at Lampwicks.)

It was fitting that it should be the cultured, cosmopolitan, knowledgeable Egon Ronay (himself the son of Budapest restaurateurs) who announced the new arrival, as it was his influential *Egon Ronay Guide* that had sent the 17-year-old Marco Pierre White on his milky way from a Harrogate hotel to the celebrated Box Tree in Ilkley. For Ronay, the discovery of a new restaurant is – deftly adapting Brillat-Savarin's famous *bon mot* about a new dish – of greater human importance than that of a new planet. (The stellar imagery seemed to be in the air: for Drew Smith, editor of the rival *Good Food Guide*, the modest establishment in the unsung suburb of Wandsworth was nothing less than "a meteor hurtling through the restaurant firmament powered by the extraordinary passion of one young man".)

It was the young man, more than the modest surroundings at Harvey's, that interested Ronay, who believed that obsession was an unmistakable sign of great chefs, "even in the bud". His name itself fascinated: "Marco the clue to his Italian mother, Pierre the clue to nothing except to the many unusual aspects of this gaunt, 25-year-old fanatic with unruly locks" who worked "inhumanly hard – an 18-hour day, until 3am".

One reason for the long hours worked by the new boy in town was, according to Ronay, his obsession with cleanliness. On a personal level at least, this, it must be said, is not a claim that would find much support among other professional observers who made their subsequent pilgrimages to the obscure former wine bar. Sharp-eyed – indeed, sharp-nosed – lady scribes in particular have felt it their duty to record such uninviting aspects of their (otherwise undeniably attractive) subject's physical appearance as unwashed, unbarbered hair, untended chin and unfastidious personal hygiene. Manicurists, it seemed, would have found ample material for hours of gainful employment.

Customers, too, many of them familiar with the traditional self-presentation of the French master chefs, must have been given pause by the fugitive glimpses of the young tyro. Those who were used to seeing the high priests of the calling – Oliver, Bocuse, Vergé, the various Troisgros and, closer to home, Raymond Blanc and the brothers Roux – in their tall toques and crisp, pristine whites which seemed just to have left the hands of devoted nuns, were unnerved at the occasional sighting of the hatless dervish in a blue butcher's apron who claimed to be the new young master of classical French cuisine.

Ronay, though, was referring to the state of the establishment, not its chef. "When he leaves, the kitchen is like an operating theatre with a difference. It has the sweet smell of success." Significantly, in the light of later developments, Ronay reported that the fledgling chef-proprietor's ambition was to own a number of popular restaurants making enough money to pour into the perfect establishment, his ultimate goal.

Today, more than a decade later, Ronay sees little reason to change his views about this "very modest man" who is "one of the most complex people I have ever met" and, with no food background, "a phenomenon". It is, he says with a Hungarian shrug, a revelation from heaven – it can't be explained. The concentration, the tension, are still there, creating a driving force that always seeks an outlet: "corked energy", as he puts it. One thing Ronay is sure of: "He doesn't do things for the sake of money." He is also convinced that "he could go very far – one only hopes he doesn't ask for too much".

Other critics followed in Ronay's footsteps to the wilds of Wandsworth. Jonathan Meades, of *The Times*, says of White, with typical robustness, that "he came fully formed: the full works". Meades remembers his first visit to Harvey's: "I had brains en gelée, followed by rabbit in langoustine sauce, and it was like the first time I read a sentence by Nabokov. I knew that this was it – the works." A A Gill of the *Sunday Times*, who arrived in a morning suit at midday, having requested an early start because he was due to attend a wedding at 3pm, found himself still at his table eight hours later. For him, White's cooking was "passionate, like receiving a love letter". At one stage he remembered "Marco rushing out with a frying pan of puy lentils, caramelized onions and foie gras, and pouring the whole lot on to my plate". "'What does it taste of?' he kept saying. 'What is it? What is it?' and I said that I didn't know. 'It's childhood,' he said. 'It's the taste of childhood.'"

"When he talks about food, it is inspirational," Gill says, "and the proof of his great gift – as close to genius as you've got – is the influence he has had on menus everywhere. I can see Marco over and over again in the restaurants I visit." Echoing Gill, Jonathan Meades says, "This guy has a kind of genius. He once told me that 'cooking is basically craft and taste – except pastry, which is chemistry': he has impeccable senses – olfactory and gustatory."

White is, as Meades puts it, the most French of the English chefs, the most Escoffier-like, the closest to the great belle-époque tradition. It was not therefore surprising – although it amazed the restaurant-going classes of London – that, as Luke Jennings reported in the *New Yorker*, "he offered a startling and sensuous menu drawn from the far extremes of the classical French repertoire. Pigeon de Bresse, for example, was stuffed with foie gras and truffles and served *en vessie* (in a pig's bladder), while noisette of lamb was presented *en crépinette* (in the filigree caul that enclosed its intestines)." Some going, for a lad from a council estate in Leeds.

Here, then, is the young maestro at his work, as discovered by Russell Miller of the *Sunday Times*, on an early visit to Harvey's: "It would not be an exaggeration to say that he looked truly terrible. His skin is etiolated and prone to pimples, his face is gaunt and his hollow eye sockets are grey. Several days' growth of wispy beard sprouts from his chin and top lip. His horrible long hair hangs over his ears in lacklustre curls apparently unfamiliar with shampoo." (He adds, more or less graciously, "For reasons not immediately evident to your reporter, women fawn over Marco. An insolent stare from the brown eyes somewhere in those sockets starts female knees weakening; his wolfish smile brings on hot flushes.")

Fortunately, "an automatic door effectively soundproofs the kitchen and protects customers' sensibilities, so who would ever guess that the sublime food served at Harvey's is created in a neurotic sweatshop fraught with hostility?" The creator of the sublime food, meanwhile, was wishing that he wasn't a cook. "I wish cooking was a passionate hobby, but it's [that word again] an obsession. I caught the bug at the Box Tree, and it's terminal. I used to dream about food – smells, tastes, textures. That must be how dishes come to me. All these ideas steam away in my head like old cabbage leaves on a compost heap, and then one day something clicks and they get translated into beautiful food on a plate."

Some of the "signature" (a food writers' buzz-word that has happily buzzed off) dishes at Harvey's came and went: the nage of sole, for instance – "I used to love it, then I got fed up with it." Fortunately for his customers, he came to love it again. Only one dish on the menu was judged perfect by its creator: the tagliatelle of oysters with caviar. "It's pure theatre to make, and it's pure theatre to eat. It has all the elements required for a good dish: there's mystery in it; it has body – both to look at and to touch, in the mouth; and the flavours are light, rich, balanced, true." Nothing, of course, is ever entirely new, as the neophyte was quick to acknowledge. "It's an original, though it has parents. One parent is at the Gavroche: huîtres Francine, an oyster shell filled with mousse. I replaced the mousse with pasta and the chives with caviar. The other parent is at the Manoir: tagliatelle of langoustines, which is simply pasta topped with langoustine tails. The marriage of these two dishes produced mine. In 30 years' time that dish will still be the same. I'm lucky to have found such a dish in my early 20s; some chefs spend a lifetime searching for a dish like that. Its elegance and its excellence make me think of my mother, so I've given it to her. It's the first dish I can really call my own, and I give it to her."*

Since the two words White would choose to describe his food are "sensuous" and "feminine", the gift seems appropriate as well as touching. "Wit" might be another ingredient of his work, as it is of his life (which he sees as the same thing). It is a factor evident in this nicely phrased piece of advice, about another Harvey's favourite, tranche of calves' liver with a sauce of lime: "Liver is a rich but bland meat, and you need something sharp to cut it – like lime. Take care with the vegetables, though: lime can upset a lot of them. Leeks get on well with lime, but a cauliflower purée, for example, would cause a lot of trouble. It would get very offended by the lime."

• • •

"Night after night," reports Luke Jennings, "Rolls-Royces, Bentleys and Porsches flattened the grass of Wandsworth Common." People from the smarter parts of town, and from baronial pads out of town,

* The recipe when published was accompanied by the phrase "In Memoriam Maria Gallina White".

were fighting for bookings – and this in spite of, or perhaps partly because of, the (reported) outrageous behaviour of the wild young chef-*patron*, who was said to have cheerfully described his customers as "fat, ugly bastards". (One new customer, Steven Saltzman, the son of the Bond films co-producer, was attracted by "the image of this wild fellow cooking this wild food". He telephoned in the impossible hope of getting a table the same night: "Sorry, full up," said the voice of Marco, definitively. Saltzman thought quickly and said, "Well, why not? I'm a fat, ugly bastard!" "Come on over," said Marco. "We'll fit you in." It was a fateful meeting: Saltzman became a regular customer and firm friend, and, through his connections in the movie world, helped decide the next change in the meteor's course.)

Those lately shaken or stirred by press reports of evictions from restaurants may perhaps regard the phenomenon as of recent origin. But the celebrated Gordon Ramsay would be the first to acknowledge his debt. Intending merely to evict a pesky critic, A A Gill, from his eponymous restaurant, Ramsay found himself with the bonus news value of throwing out with him the famous (and blameless) Joan Collins. Although admittedly adding a new twist to the procedure by ejecting his customers *before* they had eaten, Ramsay learned the art at the feet of a master, in the kitchen at Harvey's.

White explains his response (peremptory expulsion) to such "perceived impertinences" as finger-snapping at waiters or the ordering of well-done steaks. "It was ten months before I threw my first customer out. But I was like a serial killer: once I'd got the taste for it, I couldn't stop."* Adjusted figures in later years have reduced the number of ejections to a disappointing two in all, but such stories, combined with what one reporter has nicely called the young Lothario's "modelizing", were catnip to the nation's tabloid papers: a new anti-hero was born, or perhaps assembled. (The great cartoonist – and champagne connoisseur – Jak of the London

---

* "When I throw people out, they don't like it and say they are customers, but they are not customers because I have not given them a bill. They become my guests and I can do what I like with my guests." – Marco Pierre White, interview, *Today*, 9th March 1989.

Evening Standard encapsulated both failings in one drawing. It showed a "toff" prone on the pavement outside the restaurant, a snarling, cleaver-armed Marco in the doorway and a policeman to whom the customer is complaining, "All I did was ask him how his bonne femme was." Marco owns the original, the two became friends and Jak, until his untimely death, was always seated at the same table at Marco's three-star Restaurant in the Hyde Park Hotel. Above the table hung a work by the French theatre designer and painter Christian Bérard called *Carnival*. It had been painted in 1927 and the chef had discovered that that was the year of Jak's birth. It was also that of Marco's own father.

Soon newspaper readers could make their own choice between such imaginative creations as "the McEnroe of the Magimix", "the Jagger of the Aga", "the Oscar Wilde of the Wok" and "the Byron of the Backburner". Marco stories appeared in the press – as they still do

---

vignette

I was one of his first customers here. Marco is a big man – in everything: personality, outlook, also his heart. Heart as big as London! Mati is so warm-hearted too, so affectionate. And her mother is sweet! I'm alone, and they always take me out when I'm in town. I travel a lot, everywhere, but Marco cooks the best food in the world. His cooking isn't Italian or French – it's Marco! Once, I was going to the opera and asked him if I could have an early dinner. He said if I ate early I wouldn't be hungry enough for a full meal and if I ate afterwards I'd be too tired, so he said, "Look, I'll come down at five o'clock and cook you your first course, then you go to the opera and when you come back I'll cook the rest of your meal." Lovely person. A maestro! Marco never does anybody any harm.

– Mrs Maria Hunt, Italian-born, widow, opera buff, who lives in Peterborough and stays at the Hyde Park Hotel when in London

---

– almost weekly. He was, says Luke Jennings, "the *enfant terrible* of British cuisine, he was a gastro-punk lover of models and socialites, he was an egomaniacal tyrant". He adds cautiously that "there was truth in all these stories" and most particularly the last, for "the Harvey's kitchen was undoubtedly a hell-hole for White's brigade".

The pampering of the fat, ugly bastards in the front of house was undoubtedly at some cost. In White's Oak Room today, 22 chefs cook for 65 customers; at Harvey's, seven cooked for 60, and the figure was often down to two or three. (This is not counting occasions such as that when, in the hectic middle of service, the mercurial Marco challenged the young ex-professional footballer Gordon Ramsay to a 100-yard sprint to the park railings and back – Marco, of course, winning.) In the foreword to his graphic first book, *White Heat*, featuring the restaurant, White writes, "Harvey's is the hardest kitchen in Britain; it's the SAS of kitchens. But you don't get to the top by being pampered." As Jennings pointed out, "White had done eight years' hard time under the most exacting culinary taskmasters in Britain, and he saw no reason not to give as good as he got."

The photographs in the book, unposed reportages from life, were taken by Bob Carlos Clarke, and to get them he had to suffer the white heat of the kitchen himself, night after night. He had first met Marco in the summer of 1986, when he was "24 years old, handsome and sweaty like a shire stallion yet as pale and manic as a Pre-Raphaelite poet". Writing about his subject in the London *Evening Standard* magazine, *ES*, Clarke pulls no punches:

> His fervour and energy were captivating. In his kitchen he was
> oblivious to the searing of his face and forearms, or the cuts from
> crab shells and sharp knives. The restaurant was as schizophrenic as
> its despot: on one side, a bourgeois haven with the muted drone of
> compliments punctuated only by the chink of silver on china and
> glass on glass. On the other, behind a sliding plate-glass door, a
> cramped and teeming inferno, like the worst corner of a
> Hieronymus Bosch.

On a good night, when the restaurant was buzzing with salivating gourmets, Marco, like a demented scientist fuelled with caffeine and Marlboros, worked his magic on a heat-buckled oven bursting with multi-coloured flame. The whole kitchen was a hive of activity but it all focused on the space around Marco, which crackled with scalding fat and curses.

Oyster shells and iron skillets ricocheted from the white-tiled wall above the washer-up. New recruits to Marco's kitchen soon learned that the safest route to tolerable coexistence with the boss was to keep quiet and keep out of the way.

It was a sweltering evening when one young chef quietly cursed the unbearable working conditions. Across the clatter of the kitchen, Marco registered the complaint. Grabbing a razor-sharp Sabatier knife, he spun the hapless lad face-first into the wall, deftly filleted his clothes from his body, doused him with a pan of icy water, lashed him briskly with a wet dishcloth and sent him back to get on with his work with an emphatic "Better now?" I never saw that particular chef again.

Those unfamiliar with the inner life of restaurants might, to say the least, find the edge removed from their appetites by such a snapshot as the above. But to the likes of food critic A A Gill, who has worked in such kitchens, two aspects of the trade must be borne in mind. First, all good chefs are obsessional, which is just as well, because, as Gill says, "very few jobs now are true vocations, and this is one: you only make it if it is a complete obsession – from an early age". Secondly, a modern kitchen resembles nothing so much as a medieval workplace: "No other business would dare to treat its workers as they are treated in a restaurant kitchen." Yet because of the obsessional nature of the calling, it is the participants who sustain the system: any suggested amelioration to the madness of the normal kitchen tends to be opposed by the inmates themselves.

Besides, the slaves had good reason to want to cram into the galley, 18 hours a day, six days a week, poor pay or not. As Luke Jennings points out, "'Marco's boys', as the Harvey's team was known, tended to come from working-class backgrounds, like White's own. For them, the lure of the restaurant kitchen was the same as that of the boxing ring; it offered the talented the chance of becoming rich." White demanded unflagging excellence, but for those who survived, promotion was swift. He was generous with his knowledge – food writer Jonathan Meades sees him as "a brilliant trainer of chefs".

As Meades points out, though, there has been a significant social change in the kitchen personnel, entirely brought about by White (hardly surprising in view of Meades's fellow-critic A A Gill's view that the arrival on the scene of Harvey's changed the landscape of culinary Britain). Unthinkably a generation ago, middle-class and upper-middle-class boys have become, to use Meades's word, enraptured by White's contribution to cuisine. Attracted by this "Godfatherish, clannish, benevolent" despot from the working class, at least three of White's most dazzling chefs today, including the head chef of his flagship Oak Room, are ex-public schoolboys.

Tim Payne, an alumnus of the Wandsworth inferno, and today White's travelling disciple, whose task it is to spread the gospel by supervising the opening of new restaurants – lately, Quo Vadis, Mirabelle, Titanic – puts great stress on the importance of the "real relationship" he has with Marco. "He wants to know how you are, how is your family, all that," explains Payne. "There's a pretty rapid turnaround of staff in most restaurants: not here. People stay with Marco, or if they leave, come back. I could easily go elsewhere now – but I'm happy." (It should be noted that Marco, famously, pays the highest wages in the business; but it should also be noted that someone like Meades, who, as friend and critic, has known White for more than ten years, has no doubt that "he has an innate decency: he *enjoys* the people who work with him".)

Marco seems to lend support to this view: "If you look at what I've built around me, it's not because I'm a good cook, it's because I'm a leader of people." True, but he *is* a good cook. It was not because Harvey's was "trendy" (to use a word then trendy) that the eating-out classes poured from the posh purlieus of Mayfair, Chelsea and Belgravia to the wastes of Wandsworth.

The original inmates of the "neurotic sweatshop" that was Harvey's arrived there by varied paths. Some left to stand on their own two feet. Others followed in the footsteps of the young maestro. Still others left the fold and, finding the paradise of the hell-hole lost, gladly returned to it.

Lee Bunting, who had worked with Marco before, joined six weeks after Harvey's opened. He followed Marco to the glory of three stars at the Hyde Park Hotel and, 11 years on, was one of the two chefs responsible for the triumphant opening of the Mirabelle. "We know what Marco wants," he explains, with typical modesty.

Danny Crow, son of a Bethnal Green cabby and, like Marco, an Italian mother, had been the new boy's superior as sous-chef at Le Gavroche, where they were the only Englishmen in the kitchen, but he was happy to take instruction from the young leader at Harvey's. "Marco is the kindest person I have ever known. He has a heart as big as a balloon. When I went to hospital, he was the first person to visit me. 'When you come out, I've got a job for you,' he said – and he had."

Remarkably for an Englishman, Crow has been a teacher at the Cordon Bleu in Paris – for years the fief of the great Pellaprat, who taught Fernand Point and Alexandre Dumaine – and is now head chef at the handsome Waldorf Hotel in London's theatreland. He was touched when, recently, Marco abandoned a group of powerful-looking executives touring the kitchen and came over to shake his friend's hand. Granada, who have a deal with Marco, own the Waldorf. Marco will be taking over the catering, breakfast to nightcaps. The two friends will be working together again. "I'm delighted," Danny says. "I'll never let anybody talk that man down to me."

Many of White's former trainees are now important chef-proprietors in their own right, including Philip Howard, who is at the two-star Square and is co-partner with Nigel Platts-Martin, who had invited White to join him in the Harvey's venture; Jean-Christophe Novelli, of Maison Novelli; and Gordon Ramsay, late of Aubergine, now owner of the eponymous establishment in Chelsea. "You put a lot in," allows Ramsay, "but hell, you got a lot out."

The young Ramsay – today Marco's rival as the most talked-about restaurateur in the country – had happened to see an article about a new restaurant in a copy of *Caterer & Hotelkeeper* lying about in the staff canteen at the Mayfair Hotel. Five minutes later he was on the phone to Marco. "I lied to him about having experience in France, and got the job." The words tumble out of Ramsay when he recalls his time, aged 19–20, at Harvey's: words like "fascinating", "warmth", "generosity", "phenomenal energy", "creativity", "ideas" and "alive!"

"We were friends as well as colleagues. He would take me out on Sunday nights, our only day off. Then we'd go straight to Harvey's and sleep on the banquettes so as not to be late on Monday." He spent two and a half years there, "in the thick of it", learning, above all, "to *taste, taste, taste*: the palate was the most important thing in my training with Marco". Ramsay then applied for a job at Le Gavroche, and, with Marco's support, got it. In his first week there, fearing he would be late, he jumped on the Tube train without a ticket and was arrested ("so I have a criminal record") and taken to a police station, where he was allowed one phone call. He called Marco, who was furious: "Your first week! You'll lose your job!" Marco paid the £60 fine, then called Albert Roux; the job was saved. Ramsay found himself back at Harvey's, though: having borrowed £2,000 from Marco to take out a mortgage, he worked at Harvey's on Saturday nights, from 6 to 11, to pay off his debt. His one bad memory of the time was the ferocious "bollockings" (to employ the delicate language of the kitchen) for perceived mistakes or neglect, the 6 foot 3 inch wild man towering over the stocky, blond Glaswegian. "I found it hard to take," Ramsay admits. (That he can dish it out rather better than he can take it became clear to the nation in Channel 4's fly-on-the-kitchen-wall TV series that celebrated, if that is the word, the start of Ramsay's pursuit of cooking's gold medal, the third Michelin star.)

Between the fearsome inferno of Harvey's kitchen and the cool linen and calm of the restaurant, the tall, slim figure of a young Frenchman shuttled incessantly but serenely. He had arrived unannounced at the door on a rainy day – "well, it is always a rainy day in England" – after a short stay at Raymond Blanc's Manoir. Having proffered his brief CV, he was startled to find himself hauled inside by a wild-eyed, Medusa-haired, skinny giant and instantly offered the job of sommelier. (The care and serving of wine in any restaurant is as important as the quality and presentation of the food, quite apart from its value as a source of profit: in a Marco Pierre White establishment, the wine waiter may find himself uncorking a Château d'Yquem at £30,000 a bottle.)

What had blazed from the CV and fired the interest of the new proprietor, in wet Wandsworth, were the magical words "Pyramide" and "Chez Point". Here, of all unlikely visitors, was an emissary from the shrine created by the legendary Fernand Point, he whose words Marco loved to quote: "Good cooking is lots of little things done well." True, Jean-Christophe Slovik was a mere boy – 19 going on 20 – of limited experience. (He also had limited English: "I came here to improve it. In the restaurant world, one must be bilingual, and the other language must be English.") True, Point was no longer of this world, but Madame Point was, and so was Monsieur Louis, the prince of sommeliers, and so was the Pyramide at Vienne – and here was Jean-Christophe, who had sat on the restaurant's velvet banquettes and, between services, played cards with them both!

Within a week, Marco had asked Jean-Christophe to be his manager. (He is with him still: a slightly greyer version of the young man is today performing his polished art at the Oak Room, and his English is faultless.) "Marco said, 'When do you want to start – tomorrow?' He offered me three times what I was earning. I explained that I needed his help to improve my English. 'No problem,' he said."

It was hard work, Slovik remembers: "You shouldn't come into this business if you count the hours. It's a way of living. You work when others don't, eat when others don't; you are outside so-called normal life." Marco spent his life in the restaurant: "Often we would find him in the morning, sleeping in the boiler-room on the first floor – the only warm spot in the place." Harvey's didn't make money: " Marco's portions were too generous." But it was an exciting and extraordinary adventure, "and Marco had so much glamour and mystique about him – he could never be Monsieur Normal!" The tabloids were quick to pick up on this: "It was a two-way game. They needed someone to talk about at that time; they wanted spicy stories, and Marco gave them what they wanted, but a lot of what they printed was very far from the truth."

Marco, he says, was, and is, always loyal to his employees, and they to him. His genius was most apparent in the dressing of plates. "Because of my position, I was very close to this. At Harvey's he would dress *every* plate: 50 first courses, 50 main courses. Each one was impeccable. Now, at the Oak Room, he doesn't do them all himself – but I can spot a plate dressed by Marco every time!"

For Slovik, it has been a journey, as Michelin would put it, worth the detour: from the hallowed three-star Pyramide to the upstart no-star, then one-star, then two-star Harvey's, on to the three-star Oak Room – a place as close to the values and tradition of Point's Pyramide as Britain is likely to see.

Harvey's, the tangled seedbed for all Marco Pierre White's future enterprises, was more than an exacting culinary taskmaster demanding unflagging excellence in the service of undeserving fat, ugly bastards. The young Slovik was perceptive: "I never saw anyone so determined on what he wanted to do, and to always control the whole thing." This control extended from the raw materials White needed to maintain the quality of his work, to the linen on the tables – and to the flowers that stood on the starched tablecloths. Like Slovik, like the young whipping boys in the sweltering kitchen, those who met the high standards thrived and are with Marco still.

"Oh, I've been sacked, often," says Annabel Grey, a young woman of grace and charm, "but never for long." She has been choosing and arranging the flowers in Marco's restaurants for the last ten years, from

Harvey's on. Flowers, often unnoticed, are important in the creation of mood and beauty in a restaurant and, as such, receive the same unblinking, focused – well, yes, *obsessive* – attention from the master as everything else that contributes to a successful whole.

Significantly, and typically, Marco chose not a florist but an artist to perform this daily task. Annabel Grey is a designer of textiles, a painter of decorative screens ("Marco respects my painting, but doesn't like it"), a graduate of the Royal College of Art. "Marco put me on the right track. I didn't think it would last three weeks, but Marco taught me by allowing me to use his money to experiment." Some money, too: £1,000 a week was normal, and £100,000 a year at the Hyde Park Hotel showplace, where most of the flowers were imported daily from Holland.

"It hasn't always been plain sailing: there have been *ferocious* moments. Marco doesn't like yellow flowers, except for daffodils. Then when I put daffodils in The Canteen, he threw them out: he liked daffodils, but he didn't like daffodils *there*." He found a display at the Oak Room a bit showy: "You might as well put £50 notes on sticks", unconsciously quoting a barb of the critic A A Gill which had clearly found its mark. He used to like mixed arrangements but in recent years (as in the presentation of his food) he has become increasingly minimalist: a blaze of red roses here, a cloud of white tulips there. "He has taught me how to do that." His eye for the one wilting petal among a hundred healthy blooms is legendary: wary staff try to pre-empt him, but with rare success.

"Marco can behave incredibly badly at times, then he can be charming. What saves him is that, in the middle of being outrageous, he can burst out laughing at his own outrageousness." Marco gives *positive* criticism, Grey says. He has total inner confidence – and places complete confidence in those he has chosen to do things in the way he expects them to be done. "He is a very good teacher, a natural teacher. Over the years, I've seen snotty boys become men."

Back in the days of Harvey's, he was very driven – he still is, she says, but he is calmer. One morning at Harvey's, she was arranging the flowers on the tables of the apparently empty restaurant when a tablecloth moved. Marco emerged from his sleeping place, nodded good morning and headed for the kitchen.

The linen on the tables then was supplied and cared for by Colin Gershman. Today, bespectacled, be-blazered, prosperous-looking, he provides the same service for all of Marco's restaurants – and, thanks largely to his early and canny association with the young winner, for most of the capital's other top restaurants and hotels. The initiative had been Marco's, as Gershman relates:

> When he bought Harvey's, he called my office and asked if I could go to a flat, St John's Wood I think it was. There was a girl there who asked me questions, how I did business and so on. All the time we were talking, for about an hour and a half it must have been, in the background there was this tall, skinny bloke, sitting on the edge of a bed and talking non-stop on the telephone. I didn't know who he was: I had no idea what the owner of the restaurant looked like. When I got up to leave, this fellow came over and asked what price I had quoted and I told him, though it became clear that somehow he had heard everything that had been said. "You know, this could be very big, this could lead to other deals for you. If you could shave a little off that figure, I think we could do business." I could see straight away that he had integrity and good business sense. I said OK and he shook my hand and that was it.

Gershman explains that, in his trade, which operates 364 days of the year (closed Christmas Day), you are always looking for new business, and, in those days, when there were no 500-seater restaurants or celebrity chefs – hairdressers filled that role – the opening of a new restaurant, even in far-flung Wandsworth, was an event. His contract covered all linen: tablecloths (almost always white, as it makes the room look bigger) and napkins, chefs' uniforms, towels for the toilet. Marco always looked for quality, of material and of service. If anything went wrong, there wouldn't be a formal complaint but a phone call, at eight o'clock, nine o'clock at night, and the voice of Marco: "Colin, come and see me …" But Marco, he has found, is "always fair, always understanding, always listening". What's more, he pays his bills: the terror of the tabloids has always proved to be, it seems, "a highly, highly honourable man".

Another contented survivor from 1987 (with a pause: "We've just had a year off, but we're talking again") is the handsome, trim, youthful-looking Tony Allan, who went to the new restaurant to ask if he could be the chef's fishmonger, "and we struck up a close friendship". He comes, he says, from a working-class background like Marco – Allan was an Essex boy from a council estate – and neither man forgets his roots. Like others who hitched their wagon to the new star, "we grew together". Today he owns the vast and super-cool brasserie Bank (in a former bank, at Aldwych, London) and the recently opened Fish! in the old Smithfield Market. He also continues to supply top-quality fish, not only to Marco's growing empire but to London's other finicky restaurateurs. Marco and the other top chefs, Allan says, raised his standards.

"If I look back at seven or eight years of my life, it all revolved around Marco: what Marco was doing, what I was doing; my business grew as Marco grew. Marco has changed the face of the restaurant business, and I've tried to do the same in my job." This in spite of his firm belief – that of an avid and informed gourmet who has travelled extensively in France, where many of his customers are to be found – that "80 per cent of the British public don't know what they are putting in the hole under their nose". (Allan's friend Marco shares this view: "Eating and cooking food doesn't come naturally to the English. It's just fuel to the English. For the French and the Italians it's a way of living.")

Allan is a great admirer of Gordon Ramsay (who is happiest working with fish) – "he is doing incredible things right now" – but points out that "he had a fabulous teacher". Having studied both men from the early days, when Marco was "working hard, seriously hard, for four or five years at Harvey's – I watched it", Allan draws a nice distinction. Referring to the celebrated, and questionable, ejection by Ramsay of the critic A A Gill and his film-star companion, "Marco would have done it with more forethought," he says, "and Marco is big enough to take the consequences. If the two were jewel thieves, Gordon would smash the window and grab the necklace; Marco would go in like Raffles." Allan is now, like his friend, the head of a corporate food group. "He's very, very bright, Marco, very bright: he saw that there was a bigger marketplace."

For years after he had begun to supply Marco, "it was nothing unusual for him to call me at three in the morning, just to chat". (As it happened, the hour suited Allan: he would be about to set off for the fish market.) Once, at the same early hour, the two set out for a day's fishing. "I'm very good in the country, but as we were driving along, Marco said, 'Look, there's a barn owl.' I saw nothing. A little later, 'Stop the car,' said Marco, and he got out, took off his jacket, threw it over a bush, put his hand underneath – and produced a baby fox!"

It was Marco's keenness of eye and speed of action that had led to the rift between the two – that "gap year" that seems to mark a significant number of the chef's extended relationships. Allan, to his regret, made an ill-advised comment about his friend to a tabloid journalist, who saw it as manna. White – "I'm naturally litigious" – sued for libel. At year's end, the telephone rang *chez* Allan. It was Marco, wishing him a Merry Christmas. A trial date has been set, but the case may well be settled beforehand. "It was like a breath of fresh air," said the relieved Allan, sitting for the first time in the Mirabelle, which had opened during the year, and sipping a glass of his friend's champagne, before checking out the fish – his fish – and chips ("cod with pommes Pont-Neuf").

It would have been a turbot – that aristocrat of the flat fish – from Tony Allan that featured in one of the benchmark creations at Harvey's, of which its creator noted:

> This is me tinkering with another classical marriage: turbot and mustard. It was a classic that all the best restaurants did 10 or 15

years ago; it's rare now, but I didn't invent it. You can't reinvent the wheel: all you can do is put new tyres on it. The mustard gave me the sauce, and then it set me thinking about sausages, which suggested a choucroute. Then I added the shellfish. The turbot doesn't object: she's big enough to take it all. She doesn't get easily offended.*

• • •

Harvey's was a "destination" restaurant long before the jargon word reached these shores. If you wanted to go there, you had to mean it: for one thing, the owner mightn't wish to have you as a customer. Some who made it and became *habitués* (like Steven Saltzman, who lived in acceptable Victoria) claimed not to have known where Wandsworth was. Those early devotees who became friends of the emerging star have been classified by one of them, the distinguished surgeon Dimitri Yanni of the London Clinic and Harley Street, as "eccentric loners". Yanni describes himself as "a suppressed chef" and points out that "the world of cooking bears many resemblances to the world of surgery, not least the organization, ability to do things well with hands, decision-making, etc".

These "eccentric loners" were usually the kind of dedicated gourmets who, wherever they find themselves in the world, seek out those temples of gastronomy that promise an unforgettable experience. They do not want the distraction of what Duke Ellington nicely described as "people stinking up the place with talk". You might call them the non-chattering class. One member was Yiannis Kitromilides, Cypriot-born professor at the University of Greenwich. Eating alone, he attracted the attention of the young chef who, responding to his customer's evident knowledge and enthusiasm, would propose special dishes. Spotting one day that his new friend appeared untypically downcast, Marco abandoned his kitchen, led

* The recipe for turbot with baby leeks, ravioli of scallops, choucroute of celery with a grain of mustard sauce is published in *White Heat*, page 80.

him out to the backyard of the restaurant, sat him down and listened sympathetically to the story of his troubles (as it happens, a crumbling marriage). This may not be the best way of ensuring that a new restaurant thrives, but it seems as good a way as any of turning a commercial relationship into close friendship. Years later, happily remarried, the professor took his wife to the (thriving) Restaurant at the Hyde Park Hotel for a Valentine's Day dinner. Marco, a touch sleeker and dressed smartly in the whites he now deemed justified, came over to the table and said, "I hope you don't mind, but I've guessed why you are here tonight and I've prepared something special for you." It was one of those memorable meals which, for a true aficionado of the table, are an important part of the reason for living.

Richard Edwards, who had done well enough in the City to own a string of racehorses, was another of the early comers who, like truffle hounds, had scented something with an irresistible appeal to those who care deeply about the art of living well. Like many, he started as an admirer (who could well afford the cost of watching a new young master at his work) and became a firm friend. With the economic downturn of the late 1980s, things changed for Edwards. "I had no money to eat. I just turned up at Harvey's as before. It was my canteen. I never got a bill." Today, his fortunes restored, he is an almost daily visitor to the Mirabelle. Of Marco he says, "I just love the man: I'd do anything for him."

Having found in which direction Wandsworth lay, Steven Saltzman set off for what another aficionado, the film director and restaurant critic Michael Winner, recently recalled as "some narrow suburban restaurant where Marco served up sensational food that took for ever to arrive". So compelling was the atmosphere of "passion" Saltzman found there that "most Fridays and Saturdays for the next two years I would go to Harvey's just to watch him cook. There was such excitement in that kitchen – and no space, and one light-bulb!"

There was also suffering: not only physical ("Marco seemed oblivious to the cuts and burns; he was covered with welts; so were the boys, but he would never ask anyone to do something he wouldn't do himself") but also emotional. ("Marco was having lots of personal problems – breaking up with his first wife, for instance. He was stressed, angst-ridden. I was convinced he would have a heart attack.")

The food, of course, was the thing: "He had this terrific foundation of Roux, Blanc, Koffmann," explains Saltzman, "but it was here that he came into his own. I can remember the joy of Albert Roux: it was like, 'My son has come of age!' It was at Harvey's that you could see Marco deciding, 'What do *I* take from those great chefs?'"

Walking in the countryside, the two occasionally talked about their mothers. (Saltzman too had lost his mother at an early age.) "I think he always needed to show his mother that 'I'm all right, I'm doing fine.'" The cost of achievement at this level is high, and not only for the achiever. "I've been present at all kinds of tantrums – throwing people out, shouting at staff, quarrels with his wife. Marco simply can't understand why everyone doesn't aspire to the same high standards as he does.

in sickness and in health

"I was mad, I was possessed, I fired on a lot of energy. But within seven or eight years I made myself very ill." Bob Carlos Clarke, the photographer responsible for the graphic reportage on Harvey's kitchen in Marco's book *White Heat* (for which assignment Clarke prudently wore battledress), observed that "at that point, Marco was living on the edge, working in terrible conditions, pushing himself much further than anyone else would have done, living on coffee and cigarettes, sleeping under table 22 …"

Clarke was also struck by the "staggering" contrast between the violence, as he put it, of the kitchen and the delicate beauty of the product – the food on the plate. Contrasting "the Dante's Inferno" of the kitchen with "the refinement and richness" of the dishes, he found that "it was like two worlds". The one was the price of the other, and for an ambitious chef, it was a price well worth paying. The end justified the means, and the result was richly rewarded. In January 1988, Marco Pierre White was awarded his first Michelin star.

"For a 26-year-old chef to win a star within a year of opening his first restaurant was an exceptional achievement," Luke Jennings explained to the readers of the *New Yorker*:

> The Michelin universe is a rarefied one, in which far more than the food is on trial. If the napkin-folding is less than exquisite or the cloakroom's aura is negative, the establishment in question will not

be considered, and at first sight it appears curious that a high-rolling bad boy like White should have been observant of such priorities. The truth is that White's histrionics were no more than show-dressing. At heart, White, like all successful chefs (and, for that matter, all successful poachers), was, and is, meticulous.

Because, as Jennings points out, White was aware at some level that it was his outrageous self-presentation that kept him in the public eye, "he usually furnished a suitably louche display for the media". The media, generally in the form of women journalists employed by tabloid editors with their ears and everything else close to the ground, were more than willing to meet him halfway. Lynn Barber, one of the harder-nosed representatives of the genre, reported that, with the arrival of the new star in far south London, "almost immediately, the media took him up – he was *so* beautiful, and *such* good copy". Her sister scribes eagerly confirmed the young man's appeal. Caroline Phillips of the London *Evening Standard* found him "strangely compelling, with a strong presence and deliberately intimate manner. He comes over as angry, volatile and kind – probably extravagantly kind."

Megan Tresidder of the *Daily Telegraph* gamely overcame an initial rebuff: "When I phoned him to arrange the interview, I nearly cancelled it: he sounded almost psychopathic, playing cat and mouse with a simple request. He swore throughout and made offensive sexual innuendoes." She found her obstinacy rewarded: "In the kitchen later in the evening" he was "demonic, thrilling to watch, an education" and, later that night, "away from the stove, he is languid, arrogant, menacing, diffident sometimes, prone to delivering homilies".

The actress Susan George, playing a one-night stand in the sticks on behalf of the *Daily Express*, was quite overcome: "He has a disarmingly open smile that I truly feel comes from the heart. I felt that if he deigned to speak to you for a few minutes, you'd find yourself pulling up a chair to listen. I did, and I will remember this meeting for a long time."

Ginny Dougary of *The Times* had a near miss: "The first time I went to interview Marco Pierre White ... he didn't bother to turn up. This was something of a relief, since he had been so extravagantly horrible on the telephone." That was "at the tail end of Marco's heyday as a gastro-punk, when the crudeness of his manner was as legendary as the delicacy of his cooking". (By the time Marco got round to granting an audience, "his ravaged *quattrocento* face had started to fill out, the long matted locks had been shorn into a bob".)

Did he *like* women? Bob Carlos Clarke, citing his "aggression" and the fact that he "always has to be one up, ahead of the game, needs to feel he has control", is not sure. "I've never met a man who can treat a woman so badly: then he applies balm to the wound." The syndrome is brilliantly caught in Luke Jennings's vignette: "His usual tactics with female interviewers were first to appal them with his profanity, sexual suggestiveness and apparent bullying of his staff, and then to feed them – often spooning inky little baby squid or flakes of escabèche de rouget into their mouths – and be forgiven everything."

In fact, as Lynn Barber managed diligently to record, between mouthfuls, the early Harvey's years coincided with a tempestuous private life "in which he seemed to date every model in London". "Modelizing", of course, was, and is, a recognized spare-time activity of the hard-hitting, successful male (the "trophy wife" had yet to be identified and labelled), but it would be a little surprising were Marco Pierre White to be so easily categorized. For one thing, as the percipient writer Anna Pasternak observed, he had "the low boredom threshold of the perilously bright" – an accusation not readily applicable to the racing drivers, rock stars and footballers who are the traditional magnets that pull the Barbie-blonde catwalk groupies.

By the autumn of 1988, the year in which he had earlier won his first Michelin star, White was in fact a married man; his bride was the refreshingly un-modelish, pretty, hazel-eyed, blonde and petite Alex McArthur. A doctor's daughter, she was a PR girl for a south London company that supplied fish and other provisions to Harvey's. According to a friend of both, she was a "very nice", middle-class girl bowled over by the confidence and panache of this wild creature from another world. For Marco – in contrast to the model girls who had, after all, their own lives and careers and for whom, for all his celebrity, he was still only a cook – here was a biddable, well-brought-up young woman over whom he could exercise total control.

That he was, at least for a time, a devoted husband, is confirmed by his friends, the McCoys, of the celebrated Yorkshire restaurant of that name. The brothers – Eugene and Tom – hearing of a local boy who had made good down south, had gone to dine at Harvey's, admired the accomplishment of their fellow-Yorkshireman, introduced themselves, and become firm friends. On a return visit to the McCoys (who lived above their restaurant), Alex slipped on an over-polished wooden floor, breaking a leg, and was taken to hospital in Leeds. For the rest of their stay, Marco commandeered the restaurant's kitchen, prepared all Alex's meals – the McCoys remember especially a lobster creation of great beauty and finesse – and delivered them, before the astonished gaze of the hospital staff, to his young wife in her sickbed.

A child – Leticia, known as Lettie – was born but, within two years, Alex was granted a divorce, on the (to most observers) unsurprising grounds of her husband's "unreasonable behaviour". The two remain friends: Alex retains custody of the child, and the lively Lettie and her indulgent father appear to take equal pleasure in holidays at his Hampshire home, which feature frequent visits, organized by the great chef, to nearby Bournemouth for fish and chips.

In 1990, with London in full recession, restaurants that had burgeoned with the boom of the '80s closed all over town and those that survived frantically lowered their prices. Against this background, White won his second Michelin star – at the age of 28, the youngest chef anywhere ever to do so – and, with calculated panache, not only raised his prices but raised them vertiginously. The customers continued to beat a path to Harvey's door, but the pressures were increasing.

Back in the hell-hole, the driven chef was obsessively honing his skills, doing, as his master, Point, had counselled, lots of little things well. "Another principle of my cooking – and of my life, which is the same thing – is speed and rhythm," explains White. "We peak, beauty peaks, everything peaks and then it declines. In many kitchens I've worked in, stock-pots have bubbled on and on and the stocks have been ruined. I've knocked about an hour off the cooking time for veal stock and about half an hour off the time for chicken stock, to stop the flavours getting lost through over-cooking." Speed, he found, was also the secret of successful sauces: "I reduce sauces very rapidly because that's the only way to keep the flavours fresh. I put only a few drops of cream or lemon juice into a sauce at a time because it's important to taste and test each step of the way. You have to follow the development of a taste up the hill until it gets to a peak. Chuck too much in and you could send it over the side without being aware of the peak you've missed."

Had Marco reached his peak, at least as far as Harvey's was concerned? One of those assiduously attentive women journalists, Lesley Ann Jones of the *News of the World*, neatly summarized his lifestyle at the time: "He dated dangerous, leopard-skinned visions of womanhood. He insulted customers and made them pay for his autograph on the back of menus. He bullied his kitchen staff, and he charged the earth." During the summer of 1990, the year of his divorce and of his second Michelin star, White's features became so ravaged that his friend Bob Carlos Clarke, commissioned to take a photograph for an anti-drugs advertisement, asked him to model for it.

From the beginning, the strain had been almost insupportable. "I was out of my mind," remembers White. "Five months after opening I'd lost two stone in weight. If you can, imagine being panicked with pressure, day in, day out, the bank screaming at you, threatening to bounce VAT cheques. And I was 26." Although "full to bursting", Harvey's lost £50,000 in its first six months. "The most we ever took in a week there was £33,000. The only way to make serious money in my industry is volume, lots and lots of people."

Collapse, of the chef-*patron,* if not of the business, seemed inevitable. White's blood pressure soared far above a young man's normal level of 120 over 80. "The night I was taken to Westminster Hospital it was 210 over 180. Had I been an older man I would probably have died. As it is, I was paralysed down my left-hand side. In the end it went into my left foot. That's when they realized it wasn't a stroke. In fact, it was high blood pressure caused by hyperventilation."

Panic attacks, usually at night, were just one of the symptoms. The patient learned how to cope: "I'd get up, take deep breaths till the feeling of anxiety passed and I felt at peace again, then go back to bed." Whatever time he went to sleep, 50 minutes later he would be hyperventilating, and there was no treatment available except beta-blockers. He was, tests showed, allergic to nicotine and caffeine (the cause of the elevated blood pressure), a timely discovery, since "I was smoking 80 Marlboros a day – and still playing football in the park in the afternoon – and drinking a lot of coffee". With the skilled help of his doctors, his medical problems were brought under control. But there remained the matter of his tempestuous private life.

Rejected and ejected by his first wife, Marco had moved in with Nicola Barthorpe, who was PR girl to Egon Ronay's fashion-designer daughter, Edina, and, as it happened, his wife's best friend. (Irresistibly for the tabloids, Nicola had also been a schoolmate of Diana, Princess of Wales.) Shortly afterwards, Nicola ended the relationship, citing – what could hardly be denied by anyone remotely acquainted with her boyfriend's way of life – his "obsession with cooking". (In the long annals of wrecked relationships, it cannot have been often that the love rival cited is a stove.)

Deprived of a promising story, the press were soon back on the scent, announcing his engagement to a model named Susie Brookes. The papers were almost right about the engagement, but they were quite wrong about the girl. Clearing up the confusion, White announced that he was engaged to be married to another model, Lisa Butcher, whom he had met (three weeks before, according to some reports; six weeks before, according to others) outside the nightclub Tramp.

Lisa, a classic cat-walk six-footer (three inches shorter than her fiancé), was also a nicely brought-up Catholic girl, and, according to insiders, it was a combination of her wish to observe the traditional order of things and the urgency of Marco's desires that accounted for the somewhat precipitate dash for the altar. The altar in question, on a sunny day in August 1992, was that of the grand Brompton Oratory in Knightsbridge, the social apex of British Catholicism, and the best man was Albert Roux (stag-night celebrations were held in Le Gavroche). The magazine *Hello!* paid a reputed £20,000 for exclusive picture rights, and the bridal gown was an inspired creation, alas, of the most fashionable of fashion designers, Bruce Oldfield. "Alas", because, although undoubtedly eye-catching, it failed to meet the high standards of what one journalist described as "the gamey-looking bridegroom with his Wurzel Gummidge hair, sprinkling of spots and huge welt from burning fat on his wrist".

The offending dress, which the groom, conveniently forgetting his own lucrative deal with the magazine, described as "a publicity stunt", featured a plunging *décolletage* and cutaway sides. "A woman should dress for the man she is marrying. This was sexy for the world, but not for me, and I told her so." It was an ill omen. The groom, visibly nervous throughout the ceremony, later confided to his friend Luke Jennings, "When I was standing at the altar, I knew that I was making a terrible mistake." Fifteen weeks later, the couple separated, and divorce followed. (Would the marriage have lasted under any circumstances? The fearless Lynn Barber, interviewing Marco two weeks after the ceremony, asked him if he thought he could be faithful, "and he said, yes, of course, while Alan Crompton-Batt, his PR [as he still is], murmured cynically, 'Oh, for hours!'")

Whatever the effect of the notorious "Curse of *Hello!*" – relationships celebrated in its pages are thereby, in the objective view of rival publications, invariably doomed – the progress of what one observer has called "this country's great upwardly mobile culinary success story" continued, though not without its setbacks. By the early '90s Harvey's had slumped from a weekly turnover of £30,000 to a shaky £12,000. Marco Pierre White was convinced that he was going to lose his two Michelin stars: "I lost – how can I say it? – I lost my confidence and security."

It is a confession likely to surprise many who had seen only the inspired chef, the bullying boss, the tyrannical *patron* or whatever other aspect of his personality White had been pleased to present. But it was the very complexity of his character that gave rise to the many bewildering and sometimes contradictory interpretations of the man offered by acquaintances, friends and those even closer. In the four brief months of their marriage, Lisa Butcher had had time to conclude that "he seems to be about five people mixed into one, actually".

Lynn Barber, writing in the *Independent on Sunday*, was happy to offer her readers some instant analysis of "the bewildering variety of Marcos to choose from". There was "Big Chief Jaw-Jaw delivering his interminable philosophy from the wigwam" (a role, she noted wryly, that was "obviously his chosen interview persona"). There was "the pathetic lost boy whose mother had died when he was six" and, along with the "hard-headed businessman", there was "fleetingly – the cook, the creative artist, raving about the beauty of a sea-bass's skin or the shape of a lobster". Finally, and unexpectedly, there was "the unsophisticated boy recounting a recent Sunday morning's pike-fishing on Hampton Court Weir".

---

fish tales

He is fascinated by the pike, which he sees as both a predator like himself and as an embodiment of the female principle. ("Look at her," White said to me once, indicating a pike's streamlined form, baleful eye and rapacious jaw. "Wouldn't you say that was a woman?")

– Luke Jennings, the *New Yorker*

In the case of Marco Pierre White, it seems, what you get is what you see, or are allowed to see, or, more often, are enjoined to see. But, given the richness of the inner cast available to him, and given the skills and daring of the director, it would be of more than passing interest, for admirers and critics alike, to see how he would perform as he moved from the sticks on to the larger, downtown stage that was about to be offered to him.

harbour lights

Steven Saltzman believes that Marco could never have got a third star at a place like Harvey's (though Robuchon managed it at Jamin, which was no bigger, but admittedly located in the smart 16th *arrondissement* of Paris), and sooner or later a move was inevitable. There were rumours of a project in the newly developed marina complex at Chelsea Harbour. The question was, could the exquisite touch of the young master be adapted to the demands of a bigger, brasserie-type ambience and a clientele less indulgent in matters of prompt service and the whims of an eccentric chef than that of the small suburban place? At Harvey's, Marco was cooking for 35 to 40 covers; at the proposed new restaurant – to be called The Canteen – there would be well over 100, demanding an entirely different approach.

Saltzman one night took along his friend, the film star Michael Caine, who had expressed an interest in Marco's purported plans for Chelsea Harbour. Caine's interest was a professional one; although he owed his celebrity to his screen appearances, as a founder-owner of Langan's Brasserie in London's West End – for many years, *the* place to be seen – he was a restaurateur of some experience. "Everybody talks about the famous tagliatelle at Harvey's," Saltzman says, "but it was the boeuf bourguignonne – simple, classical, robust – that really expressed Marco's genius." And it was on savouring the boeuf bourguignonne, according to Saltzman, that Caine decided that The

Canteen concept would work with the wild Marco in charge. (Curiously, the boeuf bourguignonne failed to find a place in the cookbooks of either Harvey's or The Canteen.)

The Canteen's future looked full of promise. Here, after all, was a duo indisputably endowed with what Noel Coward had called "star quality". The personable Caine, on the one hand, as well as radiating the glamour that automatically attaches to famous film actors, was keenly interested in food. Having for many years been owner and part-owner of several highly regarded and successful establishments, he had garnered valuable, hands-on experience in the management of restaurants. On the other hand, here was a young chef who, within a couple of years of opening his first restaurant, had won the respect of his peers, the fidelity of his high-rolling customers, two Michelin stars for the quality of his cooking – and had acquired, while doing so, the newsworthiness and celebrity hitherto associated with the stars of rock 'n' roll. (The third partner in the enterprise, already in business with Caine, was an Italian-born entrepreneur called Claudio Pulze, who needed no persuasion: "White has inspired a new generation of young chefs and made the profession as attractive as football.") Ominously, though, unkind tongues averred gleefully that what we had here was the potential clash of two giant egos. White himself appeared to have few doubts:

> I was still very young, both in years and temperament. Meeting Michael changed my life. He showed extraordinary faith in me. He encouraged me to look beyond Wandsworth and to plan a new restaurant designed to bring top-class cooking to a level [of cost] that a wider range of customers could afford. He was willing to invest in me, not only a substantial amount of money but his time, care, advice and commitment. The lessons I have learned from him are of inestimable value.

In 1992, White sold his shares in Harvey's to Nigel Platts-Martin and a third partner. It was a critical year in his trajectory, a fact recently

confirmed by Lynn Barber, writing, with the help of hindsight, in the
Observer. "That year was the turning point, when he left Harvey's, the
restaurant that made his name, and started becoming the present
Marco, multimillionaire entrepreneur. Until then, he cared only for
cooking and winning his Michelin stars, but first Michael Caine and
then Rocco Forte opened his eyes to the world outside the kitchen."

Chelsea Harbour – a sort of pastiche marina with swank hotel,
posh apartments and chic shopping mall – is one of those soulless
enclaves for the security-seeking rich, reclaimed by avid property
developers from traditionally working-class territory. It is a type of
place more usually found abroad, in the club class of tourism with
which its inmates would be familiar from holidays in Port Grimaud
near St Tropez or Porto Cervo on the Costa Smeralda. The council
houses of Lots Road nudge the private compound, as the council
houses of Lingfield Mount had fringed the rolling, private acres of
Harewood.

The new restaurant may seem to the critical visitor today as badly
planned as the approach to it (by foot, unsheltered, around what seem
to be the backs of other enterprises). Facing the entrance, a bar leads
in to a boxing ring of tables. These are surrounded, at a lower level
(ringside, as it were), by an L-shape of more desirable tables, one side
of the "L" offering views over the tethered flashy white motor-cruisers
that seem more like exhibits at a boat show than functioning vessels.

Sight-lines to and from both areas are cunningly blocked by broad square pillars, so that one of the pleasures of restaurant-going – people-spotting – is seriously curtailed: and this in a place that was to boast not one but two celebrities on almost permanent show. (The kitchen, somewhat exotically, is on the floor above.)

It was, however, in this unpromising setting that Marco added useful skills to those he had perfected in the hell's kitchen of Harvey's. As he put it, with a graciousness he might later have regretted, in the introduction to *Canteen Cuisine** (cover: a chummy picture of the two leading lads):

> Running a successful restaurant needs two quite different skills.
> Obviously you have to understand food and be able to cook. But
> you also have to run the "front of the house", manage the business
> side, and create an atmosphere in which people can relax and enjoy
> themselves and an ambience which will encourage them to return
> and to recommend the place to their friends.

(These irreproachable observations, although sincerely expressed, would have sounded hilariously unlikely to customers of his previous establishment. Michael Winner, the ebullient film director and dedicated trencherman – and the only restaurant critic ever to pay for his own meals – had been taken by his old friend Michael Caine to "that dreadful, narrow place in Wandsworth". Waiting an hour for his dessert, he sought comfort in imagining the inspired young chef slaving over his masterpiece in the steaming kitchen. At the end of that time, Marco emerged languidly from behind a screen in the "front of the house", where he had been chatting up a likely-looking blonde.)

"Of course," Marco goes on, "the food matters enormously. But if the tables are too close together [at The Canteen they are not], or the acoustics are unsympathetic, or the décor is ugly, or the service is unfriendly, the delicious food will count for nothing. In learning

---

* *Canteen Cuisine*, Ebury Press, 1995.

about these skills I owe a huge debt to Michael." With becoming modesty, he confesses, "I suspect that if I had not met Michael Caine I could well still be cooking in Wandsworth."

The food, though, was the thing, and that famous boeuf bourguignonne had pointed the way. Marco's formation, from the age of 17, had been in the classical French cuisine, based on the finest and most expensive ingredients, to be served to no more than 60 knowledgeable customers endowed with healthy disposable incomes. Here, at The Canteen, there were a Conranesque 140 covers, and the somewhat slimmer clientele would have somewhat slimmer wallets. Portions, inevitably, would be smaller (though here caution had to be exercised: when Caine spotted an unusually tall waitress, he said, "Marco, she'll have to go – she makes the portions look small!"). The challenge of The Canteen was to bring down to an affordable level the kind of dishes served in plusher places, while keeping up the quality. The solution was that recommended by a classical master, Escoffier, no less: "Simplify, simplify, simplify." Here, for example, is Marco on one of The Canteen's most successful creations, turbot with grain mustard (a spin-off from the Harvey's dish):

Get a large Le Creuset dish, put in a knob of butter, chop your shallots, and cook without colouring. Deglaze with a little white wine and reduce for a minute or two, add fish stock, then put the turbot in, cover with a butter paper, and pop into the oven for five minutes. You've cooked it already. Pour off some of the juices, leave the fish to rest, and mount the juices with a little butter, a bit of cream to stabilize it, and a spoonful of grain mustard. It's as simple as that!

There is, of course, nothing revolutionary in the White approach. Every restaurant in France serves the same cuisine, more or less elaborately prepared. The difference between the two countries is that France has a cuisine and England does not. In that sense, the journalist who wrote that "when Marco Pierre White came south, he was in France" offered a useful insight. In fact, he had brought France with him, from the unlikely crucible of a Yorkshire kitchen and from his own creative imagination. Thus when the menu of The Canteen, though proposing admittedly "simple" fare, featured such a dish as that quoted above, it was called escalope of turbot poché. If you preferred salmon, it would be grilled darne of salmon, to be followed perhaps by magret of duck or roast saddle of lamb forestière, rounded off with a vacherin of red fruits or a nougat glacé.

The chef, according to the third partner, Claudio Pulze, was "the most influential person in the business. Ninety per cent of the people cooking today are ex-Marco. He made cooking a respectable profession. In the '60s it was hairdressers, in the '70s photographers, now it's chefs." Remaining faithful to the principles of the classical French cuisine whose secrets he had partly acquired, partly imagined, and cannily bringing with him even younger chefs trained in the hard school of the Harvey's hell-hole, the young master, cooking for some 140 covers, sensationally acquired a Michelin star. It was the biggest restaurant in the UK – possibly anywhere – to be so honoured. (Curiously, no Conran restaurant has ever achieved a Michelin star – not even the plushly bourgeois Bibendum, ironically installed in the old Michelin depot and with the roly-poly Michelin Man symbol as its decorative motif.)

To the delight of the popular press, White, it seemed, had brought with him another tradition from the wilds of Wandsworth. As even the august *Financial Times* had observed, "There are those who must imagine that to enter one of Mr White's restaurants is to stand a good chance of being grabbed by the chef-proprietor and flung into the street for some imagined slight or lapse in table manners." It is not known whether the actor Nigel Havers had any such apprehension when, as a friend of Michael Caine, he elected to dine one evening at The Canteen. Shortly after Caine had left the restaurant, word reached Marco in the kitchen that Mr Havers was complaining to the waiter. In response, Marco instructed the waiter not to bill the couple. Although the customer's grief seemed to be concerned with delays in the service, the chef, according to one of those helpful "insiders" so diligently nosed out by the press, "was furious about the complaint because Havers had eaten every single morsel of food. He tried to keep calm and just decided to give them the meal on the house. But then Havers ordered another bottle of wine – that was the last straw." Havers was asked to leave, and prudently did so.

Wherever the blame lay, all was well that ended well. Years later, unburdening himself expansively to a journalist from *Punch*, White explained: "Take Nigel Havers. I banned him after he complained about the service at The Canteen. Michael Winner acted as peacemaker. In the end, Nigel wrote me a nice note and had it delivered with a stuffed pike in a glass case. And, knowing he enjoys cooking, I sent him a book of my recipes."

• • •

The Canteen had opened in November 1992 with all the publicity that might be expected for the launch of a smart new brasserie in a smart part of town managed by a couple of smart operators who were also stars in their separate fields. Pre-tax profits in the first year topped £400,000, in the second, £1 million on a turnover of £4 million, and the desirable Chelsea location and Michelin accolade seemed to ensure its healthy future as a "destination" restaurant.

The whole thing, in fact, had been the idea of the third partner, Claudio Pulze, and he might reasonably have had misgivings from the very beginning. "Marco was strange, very strange. I invited him to lunch at Chelsea Harbour. Michael [who had a flat in the complex] came down and there was also a mutual acquaintance. Marco sat facing away, his back to me, for an hour and a half! All he said was an occasional 'yes' or 'no'. He promised to call and he didn't. Eventually we got together and he became my best friend. For four years we were very close. There wouldn't be 24 hours when we weren't in touch." He found Marco to be a skilled and determined negotiator. "I've never met anybody who was so charming. You can sit with him for an hour: if he wants something, he can switch his approach, he can produce five Marcos! At the end, he will smile, as if to say, 'You'll forgive me anyway.'"

By the third year, there were rumours of financial discord and, in the words of one journalist, "the partnership imploded". The press searched wildly for reasons. The *Sunday Times* opined that "it was all over Michael Caine's desire to introduce fish and chips on the menu". (An unlikely story: the fish-and-chip shop at the bottom of Lingfield Mount had been a favourite rendezvous of the White family, and the dish, thinly disguised as cod with pommes Pont-Neuf, is a feature on the menu at the Mirabelle.) Others, the paper suggested, said that the restaurant just wasn't large enough for both of them: "Caine was getting bossy and White became rebellious at the interference." The *Sunday Express* quoted the view of "a close associate" that "they fell out over money and ego" and added – flashing its French vocabulary – that "Michael Caine is paying Marco Pierre White, the *enfant terrible* of *haute cuisine*, £500,000 to dissolve their acrimonious partnership". Questioned on the matter, the chef's PR spokesman, Alan Crompton-Batt, responded cagily: "Marco and Michael will each tell you that they can prove they were in the right. They each believe it completely too."

In searching for the truth, it might be salutary to examine a more recent drama in the culinary world – the explosive falling-out of the same Michael Caine–Claudio Pulze partnership with Marco's former friend and pupil Gordon Ramsay (*former* friend because his continuing association with those deemed to have wronged Marco led to an estrangement lasting rather longer than the usual gap year). This time the restaurant in question was the Caine-Pulze flagship, Aubergine, in the Fulham Road. Ramsay, by dint of hard work and talent, had made the small restaurant the most fashionable in London, fully booked for months ahead and boasting two of the coveted Michelin stars. (As executive chef, he had also achieved a star for another of the group's establishments, L'Oranger in St James's Street.) Now indisputably one of the country's top chefs, Ramsay was

Gaetano Gallina, Marco's grandfather on his mother's side, photographed two years before his death in 1959. He had done well as a grain exporter in Genoa before the war, and encouraged his children to learn foreign languages.

Maria Rosa Gallina with her family, in Genoa in July 1941. Her younger brother Gianfranco (foreground) describes her as 'a marvellous girl ... who would give everything of herself'.

Marco's mother was by all accounts something between an angel and a saint, and what's more – the photographic evidence is conclusive – a beauty.

The wedding of Frank White and Maria Rosa Gallina took place on 1 June 1954. They had met at the Griffin Hotel, where he was playing cards between shifts as a chef, and it was, she later assured her son, love at first sight.

Frank White (left): a man who, one of his oldest friends said, was capable of 'starting a fight in an empty room', and whom even a loving son says was 'as prickly as a porcupine'.

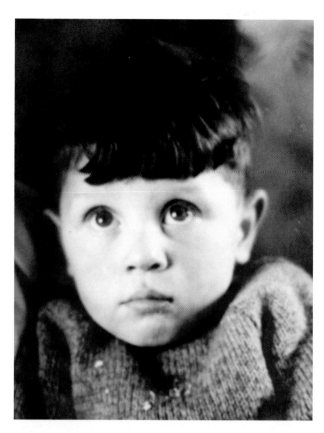

Uncle Gianfranco remembers the young Marco as 'a rather plump small boy' who was 'very, very complicated, thoughtful, strong, observant – not like the others. He studied people, and things, a lot'.

Clive and Graham White, Marco's two elder brothers, seen here in 1967, introduced him to the art of fishing at which he was later to excel.

In 1975 Marco was presented with a prize for fishing by the then Miss United Kingdom – two return train tickets to anywhere in the UK.

Winner of the Juvenile Shield for fishing, at the Bridlington Sea Angling Festival – the first of several such achievements *(photo: Yorkshire Post)*.

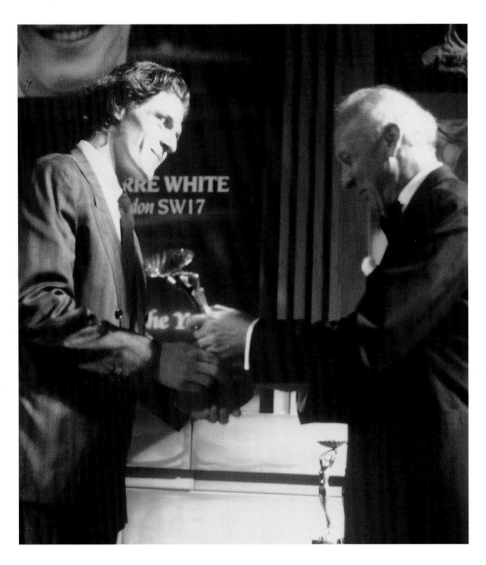

In 1987, soon after the opening of Harvey's in Wandsworth, the restaurant won the Newcomer of the Year award organised by *Hotel and Caterer* magazine, presented to Marco by Lord Montgomery of Alamein.

The archetypal 'bad boy chef', photographed at Harvey's in 1989 by *Bob Carlos Clarke*.

This cartoon by Jak in the *Evening Standard* (December 1992) perfectly conveys the popular perception of Marco at Harvey's. The caption reads: 'I only asked if his Bonne Femme was all right tonight!'

New friends. Marco and Michael Caine on a fishing trip in August 1991, shortly before they opened the Canteen together in Chelsea Harbour.

Michael Winner is an old friend (pictured here with Marco's daughter Leticia). He describes the master as 'highly talented and amusing ... also nutty, machiavellian, mercurial, utterly childish, irrational and dangerous. All qualities I greatly admire.'

The 'kitchen brigade' that helped Marco win his third Michelin star at The Restaurant in the Hyde Park Hotel. Many of them are still key members of his empire, including Charlie Rushton (at the Mirabelle), Lee Bunting and Roger Pizey.

Mati Conejero with their elder son Luciano, photographed by Mandy Foreman (née Rice-Davis) at the Berkeley Hotel.

Luciano and Marco junior on holiday in 1997 in southern Spain, where Mati's grandmother lives.

The big fish. Marco remains a brilliantly versatile fisherman – this 30 lb pike was caught in the Avon in Hampshire in 1999.

Marco and one of his key mentors, Albert Roux, celebrating Albert's birthday in the Grill Room at the Café Royal in 1997.

Since formally announcing his retirement from restaurant cooking, Marco has found new enthusiasm for cooking at home. Among his other favourite occupations are shooting (top), and making works of art comparable to those of his erstwhile friend Damien Hurst (above).

understandably eager to focus on achieving the magic third star for Aubergine – an ambition apparently in conflict with the plans of his associates. Publicly and vociferously announcing his refusal to be party to a brand-stretching operation that would use the restaurant's respected name "for a chain of pizza joints", Ramsay stormed out in July 1998, taking his staff (from both restaurants) with him. "They did the same thing to me as they did to Marco," he claims. His former partners are suing for damages in a considerable amount. Meanwhile, in September Ramsay opened his own, eponymous restaurant and retained his two stars. Not being privy to the accounts and marketing plans, the observer can only speculate on the motives of businessmen apparently so ready, not once but twice, to kill the geese that lay the golden eggs.

What is certain is that, in the case of White *v* Caine, neither of the principals is talking, and for good reason. A court settlement was imposed that forbade either party ever to speak of the affair again. They may, however, be talking to each other again before long. Having to choose, as in a divorce, between the two warring parties, Michael Winner, who had been a friend of Caine's since 1953, ceased to frequent Marco's establishments, much to his regret ("he is wonderful company"). Recently, though, having sprung to Marco's side in an hour of need, Winner persuaded him to write, in placatory terms, to his former partner. "Marco, being a decent chap, did so; Michael, also being a decent chap, responded in kind. So we all resumed relations," explains Winner, "and I was going to take Michael to the Mirabelle, but he had to go to America to make a film."

If Harvey's had been the first tremulous step on the road to culinary stardom, The Canteen was a major turning point in the career of Marco Pierre White. But whereas life in the hell-hole had threatened his health, he emerged from the turmoil of the battle of Chelsea Harbour a stronger man. Twice a day he would cook – on Saturday nights, with multiple sittings, for up to 400 covers – to Michelin-star standard. This, given the strains to which the beleaguered chef was subjected, was in itself a remarkable achievement: no British restaurant of similar size had ever won the Michelin award, and The Canteen retained its pulling power as a cheerful "destination" restaurant in the otherwise glum precincts of Chelsea Harbour. The daily pressures, though, eventually took their toll on Marco, and stories began to circulate in the press about legal proceedings and injunctions against his partners and their accountants.

Hayley Edwards, a notably calm and well-balanced young woman (qualities essential to her current job as manager of the Criterion), worked with Marco not only at The Canteen but, like him, at the burgeoning Restaurant at the Hyde Park Hotel, where, as PR, she shared a cramped office with the embattled chef. She has vivid recollections of the effects on Marco of the pressures of that time: the ten-fold increase in coffee consumption, the pale and blotchy complexion, the deterioration of his normally firm but polite manner with his staff. "But he never let up," she says. "He's really single-minded when he believes he is in the right." Marco was to endure two years of legal warfare with his partners, their accountants and their lawyers, spending hours each morning, before kitchen service, consulting law books, looking up esoteric legal terms in the dictionary.

All-too-human jealousy, he might have felt, justifiably or not, may well have been a factor in perceived attempts by his erstwhile friends to present the figures in a way unfavourable to him. As at Harvey's, *he* was the magnet that drew the crowds that packed the restaurant (on a recent, post-White, Friday-night visit, no more than six tables were occupied). He, and not the famous actor with ambitions in the restaurant field, or the anonymous entrepreneur, had become the star. "Who does he fucking think he is?" Caine was reported to have asked a mutual friend. Of his Italian colleague, Marco demanded, "Name one other restaurant he's had anything to do with." (Marco has claimed that, at the start of negotiations, Caine had asked him, "Do we need the Italian?") In the end, the known facts are that Marco parted company with Caine and Pulze in a court settlement that, as has been noted, forbade the parties from talking about it. Indeed, White adamantly refused to do so to this author. Since the terms of the agreement were not made public it is unlikely that they will ever be known. But for all the stress and turmoil, inner and outer, Marco clearly emerged from the ordeal a wiser, and a richer, man.

To add to the stresses of the period, White, still embroiled in his precipitate and ill-starred second marriage, had a new girlfriend, a young Spaniard who had joined the staff of The Canteen, and she was expecting his child. "I didn't break up the marriage," says Matilda Conejero, known as Mati, and few who recalled the bridegroom's own misgivings at the altar, or knew Mati, would question her honesty in the matter. In Michael Winner's opinion, "He is very lucky to have Mati. It's a miracle that he found her. He might have gone over the edge without her."

The miracle was that they had met at all. Mati, a fine-boned, auburn-haired beauty with a model's figure but also a brain, had arrived at The Canteen by chance. Born in Majorca, the product of an upwardly mobile southern Spanish working-class family, and speaking a faultless upper-class English acquired at the Convent of the Sacred Heart in Hammersmith, London, she had spent a couple of post-school winters in France, the summers with her family in Spain. Arriving back in England with no particular qualifications or plans, and needing to find employment, she had bumped into an old acquaintance. He was, he told her, to be manager of a new restaurant, about to open, in Chelsea. Perhaps there would be a job for her there. She was bright, personable, bilingual and a willing worker. When the restaurant opened, in November 1992, Mati was a member of the new team that would run it.

Shortly before the opening, she was standing near the entrance of the still-unfinished building when the works foreman walked in, accompanied by a tall, good-looking man. She knew nothing of the London restaurant scene, or the celebrity chefs who peopled it. She had never heard of the famous Marco Pierre White. All she knew was that this man produced "a funny feeling, an impact in the pit of my stomach". She hoped he would not speak to her because "I wouldn't have known what to say". The word "charismatic", so often employed in descriptions of Marco, is not a word she likes. "It has a suggestion of shallowness, but Marco has *presence*. He also has this theatrical quality – and great strength." She had, she claims, no specific intentions: "I just thought, 'What a man!'"

The tall stranger said nothing: perhaps he was having thoughts of his own about the stunning Spaniard. They spoke a few days later, when they found themselves side by side, washing cutlery in the kitchen. Mati had been put in charge of the bar that faces the entrance to The Canteen: "I was the best bartender in London." An intrepid reporter from *Hello!* magazine, that acknowledged authority on celebrity liaisons, noted, "Three days after the conversation became more meaningful, Marco turned up on her doorstep with a bag of dirty washing. 'He had noticed I had a washing machine. He never misses a thing.'"

He was, she says, "the first man I had met who knew where he was going". She found him "incredibly sensitive – I used to worry so much about doing something wrong – and incredibly generous-spirited". Anyone – lowly commis or whatever – could call on him at any time; "he'll do something about it: that's why he has such a loyal staff". Mati's appeal to Marco went beyond the obvious attractions of a beautiful, exotic girl with a shapely figure: there was no shortage of that brand of pulchritude among the boutiques and watering-holes of Chelsea. What drew him to her, apart from a dress sense that met his high aesthetic standards (a constant anxiety of hers at the beginning of the relationship), were her intelligence and her strength. "She's a strong woman," he told his friend Luke Jennings (who noted that the new girl "does not stand for any monkey business"). "She keeps me in line."

Friends unequivocally approved of the new relationship. (The almost instant marriage to Lisa Butcher had been almost as rapidly terminated.) "Very few people could manage him," says Michael Winner. "She's a wonderful influence, a wonderful woman." He observes, however, that Mati, too, has a volatile nature: "It's a fiery

fish tales

He fishes like an angler on speed, pacing manically up and down the weir in his green wellies.

– **Ginny Dougary,** *The Times*

relationship!" Today, he points out, the daily round for the reformed Marco is composed of "family life, fishing, work".

In December 1993, a son, Luciano, was born. Eighteen months later, a second son, Marco, arrived. The family now divides its time between a flat in Knightsbridge and the house on the River Avon in Hampshire. (The flat is soon to be abandoned for a roomier property in the equally snooty but more residential Holland Park. It will be nearer to the children's school and to the home of Mati's mother, a shy and caring lady who, according to her daughter, "thinks Marco has a very fiery temper but says she's never met anyone with such a big heart".)

• • •

Well before the Chelsea Harbour battle, Marco had found other, and bigger, fish and chips to fry. In spite of the stress and indignities of the business break-up, White freely acknowledged that he had reason to be grateful to Michael Caine, for at least two reasons. First, Caine had revealed to him a larger, potentially more profitable world than that encompassed by the converted wine bar in Wandsworth. And, second, Caine had introduced Marco to Rocco Forte (now Sir Rocco Forte), chairman of the country's biggest hotel chain and son of its Italian immigrant founder, Lord Forte. (This was following an initial, failed rendezvous, described here by Forte: "My friend Michael Caine had invited me to The Canteen with the intention of introducing me to Marco. As soon as we sat down, Michael said, 'Sorry about this, but you won't be able to meet the chef tonight. He's over there, having dinner with our Spanish barmaid and her mother. He's made the girl pregnant and they're sorting it out.'")

Once contact had finally been made, it was to lead the still-young, largely unschooled chef not only to the peak of his profession but also to the panelled and cigar-scented boardrooms of the power-brokers. As a close observer of Marco's progress, Matthew Fort, food editor of the *Guardian*, noted, "It is as if, from the moment he established Harvey's in Wandsworth in 1987, he set out to make himself rich – secure, he would say – and has followed that ambition with unswerving determination ever since." On the way, he was to make culinary history.

grand hotel

Once upon a time in London (and in Paris, Vienna, Budapest), a night out on the town meant dinner, and probably dancing, in one of the ornate, rococo dining rooms that were the imposing centrepieces of all the grand hotels. César Ritz, as ever seeking only the best, put Escoffier in charge of the restaurant of the Savoy and turned it into the social hub of London. Those, of course, were the days before mass tourism, when things were more ordered, the social calibre of the clientele more elevated. Guests arrived, not piecemeal and holiday-clad at all hours from the airport, but manageably together, often with their servants, off the Pullman and wagon-lit carriages of the boat-train.

But, as the journalist Emily Green graphically put it, by the late '80s "hotel dining rooms were dead". The demise was, naturally, of some concern to hoteliers, among them Rocco Forte, the chairman of Britain's largest hotel chain. As Green explained, "All the 'food and beverage men' and 'executive chefs' and 'central buying' experts his corporation could employ couldn't get sexy food on the table, or a decent buzz going."

In the more measured language of the *New Yorker*, Forte's problem seemed "intractable". "His hotel dining rooms were losing money. The grandly formal halls had been all but deserted in favour of sexier, more intimate 'houses' like Harvey's." Consequently, it was not just White who was grateful to Michael Caine for the introduction to Rocco Forte. Forte had cause to be grateful too. It had occurred to him that if he were to sublet his dining rooms to the new, star-name chefs, of whom Marco was the acknowledged leader, he might just win back a fashionable clientele.

Forte's Hyde Park Hotel is situated in one of the great social 'n' shopping hubs of London, along with Harvey Nichols (which had been favoured by the Princess of Wales) and Harrod's (patronized by the Queen). It was endowed with two dining rooms: the airy, park-view space on the first floor, and the Grill Room, which shared its kitchen. The Grill Room possessed an obvious advantage: it had a street entrance. This not only obviated, for the more sensitive clientele, the intimidating ordeal of having to brave the hotel lobby and its inquisitorial stares, but also offered the possibility to the management of creating a distinct identity for the establishment.

France's top chef, Alain Ducasse, had shown the way. He had recently demonstrated at the Hotel de Paris in Monte Carlo that, with a separate entrance and a distinguishing name, it was possible to create, within a hotel, a restaurant that was not only economically successful but, for the first time in the history of the *Michelin Guide*, one worthy of three stars. It was a lesson not lost on Marco Pierre White, the star chef to whom Rocco Forte, in an unprecedented deal (though with Michael Caine still around as a minority shareholder), had leased on favourable terms the old Grill Room of the Hyde Park Hotel. (Reaction of the *Independent on Sunday*: "The 35-year-old chef is, it appears, the company's strategy on two legs. Whether this is wise or not depends on whether you think Marco's mad. Many do.")

Mad or not, Marco now found himself with one of the most desirable and fashionable locations in the chic heart of London, at a modest rent and with the right to keep all the profits. State-of-the-art

---

vignette

It's very difficult to promote quality restaurants in hotels, to get people to come. I have great respect for Marco: a genius as chef, and a very clever businessman. I was also quite impressed with the improved turnover at the Hyde Park on Marco's arrival: from something like £600,000 a year to more than £2 million.

– Sir Rocco Forte, former chairman of the Forte hotel chain

kitchens were built on the ground floor, and the room lavishly redecorated. The name for the new place was not far to seek, though some commentators found it a mite portentous. In September of 1993, emblazoned in white on royal blue on a New York-style awning protruding from the red-brick Edwardian facade, the legend "The Restaurant – Marco Pierre White" greeted the bemused gaze of the shoppers and denizens of exclusive Knightsbridge. (Marco, driving by with Mati to see his name for the first time in lights, so to speak, was initially silent; when he spoke, it was to say, "If only my mother could have been here to see that.")

Michelin, in a rare gesture of confidence, allowed the chef to keep the two stars he had earned as a debutant at Harvey's. The rest would be up to the likely lad from the council estate up north. As one observer noted, "As far as White was concerned, Wandsworth had been about playing the volatile rock-star chef; this was business."

"When I first heard that Marco Pierre White had joined forces with Lord Forte, I thought it was one of the wittiest jokes ever, for it was like chalk joining forces with cheese, or the bull joining forces with the china shop." The chortler, writing in the *Sunday Times*, is Craig Brown, one of those sit-down comedians engaged by British editors to cut waggish capers for the distraction of readers who, they fear, might be bored by the serious reporting of culinary matters.

Unlike the suspicious press, Rocco Forte – an engaging, decent, charming and elegant man who had developed a friendly relationship (which continues) with his new partner – had great respect for Marco Pierre White, and not only for his culinary prowess. "He is a genius as a chef, and a very clever businessman." Marco was also clearly not easy to deal with, and not an organization man. "He gave executives a hard time – but that didn't bother me." Forte knew how difficult it was to promote quality in a hotel restaurant. Yet, as Emily Green observed of the Hyde Park, there was potential too: "These palatial old premises, with their posh addresses and all that marble, enhance a sense of occasion." Forte saw that Marco was clearly excited by the challenge, but also saw that he now had the stature and confidence to meet it. Marco had always put on something of a front – "a bit of a game" – but he was becoming less inclined to do so. He had always shown humour, wit, a sense of naughtiness, but, according to Rocco, with his new-found domestic stability "he was much more serious than he was, even two years ago". (Rocco's faith was to be more than justified ... and repaid. When the Forte empire was eventually wrested from him, Rocco – whom Marco refers to as "the only man who ever gave me everything he promised" – had to start again from scratch. "Marco recognizes a favour. I helped him, now he wants to help me.")

Freed from the financial constraints that had limited the possibilities at Harvey's, Marco turned his attention, not to the cuisine – he had proven ability, and a faithful staff had followed him – but to the ambience of the new restaurant. Unobserved by even the beadiest-eyed tabloids, the more serious new Marco – himself an acknowledged master of visual presentation on the plate – had also been spreading his wings in the world of art (his favourite and best subject as a dyslexic pupil at Fir Trees Primary). He filled the room with works from his own collection of early twentieth-century paintings by Gertler, Berard and Gluck (described by Craig Brown as "some of the most hideous paintings I have ever set eyes on") and sculptures by Bugatti. On and around the widely spaced tables, that other artist, Marco's friend Annabel Grey, lavished lilies at a liberal £1,000 a day.

There was also the furniture. "During the next few weeks at the Hyde Park, everything changed over 95 times." Were it any other client, says the antique dealer Keith Skeel, sitting in his oaky Islington emporium, he would have told him to get lost. "But Marco had a feeling. He knew where he was going. And he had enormous charm." He was never satisfied, Skeel says; perfectionists never are.

Skeel's assistant had said one day, in a carefully neutral tone, "Would you like to meet this cook I know?" Shortly afterwards, Marco had walked into the shop with his decorator, having clearly already been to many other places. It was the beginning of one of those complex relationships in which Marco seems to specialize. After much moving out, and moving back, of furniture, pictures, *objets d'art*, Marco invited Skeel to dinner. "He takes stock, tests you out, like a matador, probing for weaknesses – and strengths." A firm rapport was established, they talked three or four times a day and, as happens in Marco's entourage, went fishing. ("Nothing *organized*, of course: it's always 'I want it now' with Marco.")

"He knew nothing about my field, but he is probably the fastest learner I've ever met. It's frightening. He asks questions, pays incredible attention." Skeel also noted "an amazing sensitivity there. One day at the hotel, I was very upset about something in my personal life. I didn't think it showed, but Marco stopped what he was doing and took me for a walk in the park, sat me on a bench and let me talk about my problems for half an hour or more. How many people would take the trouble? He has great generosity – the ability to give of himself. He's unique."

Skeel contends that "Marco's passion is not food, but people – he happens to be a cook, but could have been anything". However, he allows that "Marco's restaurants are very much here and now – not faded glory: classical, but here and now. One of the marvellous things Marco has done is to bring a lot of light into the restaurant area. London was grim – Marco is the main person responsible for the change."

The change at the faded old Grill Room of the Hyde Park Hotel was immediately appraised by the critics. Noting that the Hyde Park Hotel had long been a cornerstone of the Forte empire, that the Queen and Princess Margaret had attended dancing classes there, that Rudolph Valentino had been a regular guest and that whenever Mahatma Ghandi had stopped by, a goat was milked each day, Craig Brown of the *Sunday Times* found The Restaurant "an odd sort of place". In view of Marco's unerring eye, it was perhaps unfortunate that "our own table was situated under a painting which contained a bright yellow quince on bright purple silk, set against a yucky Barbara Cartland landscape". Although "like The Canteen … The Restaurant has a curious feeling of restlessness, as if it could be in any hotel in any part of the world", he conceded that there were "areas of pleasantness: the up-market rush-matting floor lends it an unstuffy feeling [and] there is plenty of space between tables". Brown added graciously that the staff "except for a somewhat po-faced wine-waiter" were "easygoing yet scrupulously efficient".

That doyenne of the London restaurant critics, Fay Maschler of the *Evening Standard*, found that the price ("a defiant set sum of £80 per person") brought with it "the trappings of luxury, including widely spaced tables in an area more like a drawing room than a dining room" and "formal service amiably led" by the French *maître d'hôtel*.

Emily Green, something of a Marco groupie since his earliest gigs, was pleased to report in the *Independent* that "Mr White has assembled a romantic, luxurious setting which is one of the few in London that are neither gloomy nor frilly. Just handsome." The waspish A A Gill, for the *Sunday Times*, noting that "Marco is not someone who spends money quietly", was full of praise for the expensive amount of "creamily opulent" space provided, though he commented that the centrepiece was a "huge display of flowers that rustle with all the humility of £50 notes on sticks". (In a nice irony, the criticism from Gill, a graduate of the Royal College of Art, was of a fellow graduate of the college, Marco's florist Annabel Grey.)

The magisterial *Times* man, Jonathan Meades, ever willing to share his polymathic learning with his readers, reported that "The Restaurant is rather different to what one might have anticipated after Harvey's and The Canteen. It is surprisingly staid and muted. There are some good paintings and some fine pieces of furniture, but the overall feel is of a room that is determined not to offend. It is spacious, soothing and self-consciously indifferent to fashion." Echoing Craig Brown, Meades added, "There seem to be as many staff as there are customers; the entire population of some small French town works here." But can the wine-waiter – "a grave young sommelier advises with some charm" – possibly be the same "po-faced" chap who had displeased Brown? Brown himself was happy about one thing. Having evoked the dreaded image of "Marco Pierre White, the wild man of *haute cuisine*", he was pleased to report that he and his dining companion "got away without a fight and who can ask for anything more?"

Décor matters, and for White, vitally: "There should always be something happening to engage the eye." But food, and the wine that best marries with it, is the *raison d'être* of a chef's life, and at The Restaurant, much was at stake. There was the Forte bottom line: could the rising young star reverse a seemingly implacable trend and turn a money loser into a profitable venture? There was also the matter of the dazzling performer's career: he had been talent-spotted in the sticks, he had had his chance, so to speak, off-Broadway and shone (surviving mortal combat with another star); now he was launched on the Great Marco Pierre White Way. Critics, they say, can make or break a production, but they don't hand out the Emmys and the Oscars. That, for any ambitious chef, is the role of the *Michelin Guide*, which has the award of the covetable three stars in its gift. And, apart from the glory it bestows, the cachet of three stars, as has been amply proved, brings in the customers.

• • •

Opening night, in September 1993, was a disaster, according to Michael Winner who, sensibly enough, thereupon vowed never again to review a restaurant until the chef and staff had had time to settle in. Things began badly when the waiter dropped a floury bread roll down the front of the snappy blue serge suit of Winner's dining companion, the fastidious Michael Caine, and got worse when the first course took an hour and a half to arrive.

When the food did appear, it was, to nobody's surprise, classical French in inspiration – "very grand, very formal", according to the *New Yorker*. It noted that "the menu bore the dates that White had perfected each dish (a detail that was rather too exquisite for some commentators)". Indeed: of this quirky innovation, Fay Maschler mused, "It is either an exhibition of *folie de grandeur* or a bid, similar to the one made by French chef Jacques Maximin, to 'copyright' recipes." Jonathan Meades found it "a device which might seem slightly pompous"; on the other hand, he said, "It certainly indicates the caution with which White proceeds. Everything is doggedly rehearsed, nothing is left to chance." To Craig Brown, it was "a self-congratulatory gesture made all the more absurd by the pathetically small range of years, the earliest being 1987, and the vast majority being in the 1990s" – rather as if Marco Pierre White, barely out of his 20s, should somehow have arranged to be born earlier. In fact, Marco had dreamed up this device to distract customers and critics from the fact that he had not had time to create new dishes for the opening.

What the young chef himself had in mind for this, his apotheosis, had been long made clear by the man himself. What he cooked was, had always been, classical French cuisine: an amazing act of observation, imagination and re-creation for a Yorkshire boy whose knowledge of France, even now, is confined to a day trip to Paris, whose culinary high point was reportedly a cup of coffee in La Coupole. There was only one snag: his clientele, inevitably, was largely British, a fact that he had acknowledged earlier in his career with the youthfully brash observation that the French and Italians knew how to eat but the English didn't.

Things might not have changed in that respect, in spite of his prodigious efforts and those of his peers, but *he* had, or at least his attitude towards the facts had. "In France, because of the different food ethos or culture," he stated, with (considering the circumstances) breathtaking authority, "the great chefs can get away with offering a simple roast chicken, grilled sea bream with a red wine sauce or salmon with a sorrel sauce. That cutting through to the essentials is something I'd like to do as well, but nine out of ten of my customers wouldn't understand it." (The contemporary French attitude has been nicely encapsulated by the respected Jean-Marie Amat of the stunning

St James outside Bordeaux: "A dish reaches perfection when all that is not absolutely necessary has been discarded.")

"There is a different mentality in Britain," White noted, "and thus I have to give them more to look at on the plate, and more to actually eat. I'd prefer not to serve anything with my salmon and tapenade, for instance, but I'm in a service industry and, to a certain extent, what the customer wants and expects, I have to respect. Chefs should not really be telling people how to eat." It is against this philosophical background that the views of the professional critics of the more thoughtful newspapers, whose readers form the actual or potential restaurant clientele, should be examined. (Not surprisingly, as will be seen, Marco Pierre White has his own, typically trenchant, views of those critics' views.)

With typical flamboyance, A A Gill of the *Sunday Times* invited a couple of heavies to lunch: the portly politician Nicholas Soames and the roistering rent-an-editor Andrew Neil. Also typically, in a review of 1,367 words, he devoted a single paragraph of 120 words to the food – which is, of course, any eatery's reason for existence and hence of no small interest to the reader. These few words, however, are full of praise, conveyed in his trade-mark razzle-dazzle prose: "impossibly sweet scallops in a coulis of cabbage and ginger"; a rather baffling "small cup of fish soup that was more intensive than a French starlet in a black-and-white thunderstorm"; a "gobsmacking" ballotine of wild salmon with a salad of crayfish and "a dollop of caviar"; the rabbit in a risotto with asparagus is "as tender as a mother's goodnight kiss", the asparagus "priapic".

Thankfully removing his hyperactive tongue from his sheer cheek, and disarmingly undercutting his own hyperbole, Gill blames the accomplishment of the cooking for transporting a romantically inclined writer into scribbling "a warm pink custard of cringing hyperbole, sprinkled with sugared clichés". For, he dutifully reports, it is "the technical stuff that makes Marco a great chef. He dedicates an inordinate amount of time, and the energy of his 17-strong brigade, to the mechanics, chemistry and physics of cookery. The dishes are beautiful without being prissy. The flavours harmonize but remain singular and surprising. From the first time I ate in his kitchen at Harvey's, years ago, I can't remember a dish that wasn't sublime." So sublime, indeed, that "if I were a condemned man, I'd want Marco to cook my last meal".

The great man himself joined Gill for coffee (they are good friends) and left him with a nice digestif to round out his piece. "You know," he said, "it's exactly 18 years to the day since I first started work in a kitchen. I remember the chef came in with some bags of peas to be podded and I said, 'Chef, do you know what 14 bags of peas look like when they're podded?' and he said, 'No.' So I threw away six of them. That's when I realized I probably wasn't the same as other cooks."

Noting that "the plates bear the chef's name as surely as the food bears his 'signature',", Jonathan Meades (whose own "signature" is a knowing mix of the academic with the demotic, seasoned with gusto) reported for *The Times* that "The Restaurant's foie gras terrine is as good as you'll get: it is less overwhelmingly rich than White's earlier version". More progress elsewhere: "Braised pig's trotter is another dish that has, seemingly, been amended: it could never be described as 'light', but this year's model is more delicate than the original." "The finesse of this cooking is total," Meades concluded, giving special praise to the desserts of Roger Pizey (whom Marco had brought with him from Harvey's, and who is now at the Mirabelle) – "just about the top *pâtissier* in town". Unlike Gill, long a stranger to alcohol, Meades has a cautionary word of praise for the wine list: "37 pages long, persistently impressive, persistently expensive". The 1966 Petrus, listed at £490, was "like liquid herbs" but "there are actually a number of more affordable bottles, such as the excellent Provençal Château Simone and the Pauillac cru bourgeois Château Pibran". Meades gave White a mark of 9 out of 10; after a later visit, following the establishment's transfer to the Oak Room at the Meridien Hotel in Piccadilly, he amended this to 10 out of 10.

As if to demonstrate to A A Gill that food may be evocatively described without self-conscious giggling, the faithful follower Emily Green, of the *Independent*, caught up with "Mr White, the youngest chef ever to win two Michelin stars, the cook with rock-star good looks and short-lived marriages", still trailing his clouds of earlier glory. Settling, on grounds of cost, for the set lunch, she started with "perhaps the best of his dishes: escabèche of red mullet with pickled onions and carrots. There was always saffron in it; now there are fields of it. The dish has every taste one can register: sweetness from the carrots, sourness from the vinegar of the marinade, smokiness from the saffron and a salty, sea-fresh hit with small dabs of caviar around the plate." This savoury morsel was, however, "trumped" by quails that were "the first and only ones, I now realize, that I have eaten properly cooked". The two quails – "one [on its own] looks too small," according to White – were "moist and flavourful, with a crisp skin", the sauce dominated by "a light, perfumed sense of honey, of muscat grape". Dominating the menu, though, was "Mr White, quoting an even bigger egotist than himself, Salvador Dali: 'At six I wanted to be a chef, at seven, Napoleon, and my ambitions have been growing ever since.'"

Given the limited parameters of her patch, her length of service and the fact that she also edits her paper's restaurant guide, it is hardly surprising that the London *Evening Standard*'s cultivated Fay Maschler knows the city's restaurant scene better than any other reviewer. Her probity, and perhaps her sex, together with a certain sly humour, save her from the occasional pomposity and vacuity perpetrated by her mostly male rivals. Of The Restaurant, she wrote in October 1993 that she had eaten "the best meal of this year". Maschler slightly takes the glow off this tribute with the subsequent comment: "White's prodigious talent at the stove and his ability to teach, combined with sometimes defective social behaviour, bring to mind a kind of idiot savant." Agreeing with Emily Green, she found the soup of red mullet "sublime in the force of its flavour". The terrine of foie gras en gelée was "a slice of smoothness which my companion described as 'magic butter'". Those were unbidden offerings from the famously generous chef: of her real starter, a salad, she reported that "the lobster was tender without being soft or vapid, the potatoes, having been boiled in stock, were salty but not overbearingly so, and the amount of black truffles might have pleased even Colette, who demanded that they always be 'served in munificent quantities'". (She might have added that the French writer also quipped that the right amount of truffles was too many.) Vinaigrette of leeks and langoustines was "stunningly good" (though the basic idea, she claims, was Pierre Koffmann's) and the desserts "impeccable". The wine list was "a noble one but mark-ups may deter building on what is already a whacking cost for food" (a complaint common to all the reviewers).

Out of an 82-line review in the *Independent*, Craig Brown devotes just eight lines to the food, and puts most of the comments into the busy mouth of his dining companion, a Mr ("I've never seen the point in food") Donaldson. "His magical meal consisted of a tiny bowl of unbelievably tasty mushroom soup, a 'very, very, very good' délice of salmon homardine ('heaven knows how he does it') and a blackberry soufflé ('the best of all'). Donaldson particularly enjoyed the absence of any vegetables. 'They had the good manners not even to suggest them. Who wants ghastly veg on their plate?'" Brown's personal report had at least the merit of brevity: "My own food [listing his three courses] was certainly nothing to sniff at."

It is hard to believe that such vacuities and fatuities can have been assumed to be the preferred diet of his readers by the editor of the classy *Independent*. (The editor of *Le Figaro* would know better.) More importantly, whatever may be one's view of the importance of good food, they hardly do justice to the calibre of those working 16-hour days to perfect it. As well as "The genius that is bad-boy White" – the *Evening Standard*'s headline – and his talented *pâtissier* Roger Pizey (a former shepherd, trained by the great Gaston Lenôtre at his base in the aptly named village of Plaisir, outside Paris), the brigade at The Restaurant contained such budding talents as Charlie Rushton and Robert Reid. Rushton is now head chef at the thriving Mirabelle, and

Reid is custodian today of the precious three Michelin stars at the Oak Room.

It was perhaps in defence of such loyal servants that Marco Pierre White turned his considerable firepower on the nation's restaurant reviewers, using the handy platform of the introduction to his *Wild Food from Land and Sea*,[1] launched at the Hyde Park Hotel in 1994:

That's what I dislike about food critics, whether in magazines, newspapers or food guides, this lack of true insight into what we do, this blinkered attitude. Very few of them have undergone the long, exhaustive and exhausting years of training we have, yet they feel licensed to pontificate about restaurants, food, chefs and their cooking, sometimes destroying a hard-won reputation overnight. Far too often their reviews reveal to us chefs just how *little* they actually know about food.

There are only a handful of critics whose opinions I respect – they have been around a long time, they have eaten in enough establishments, and are good cooks themselves.[2] But sadly there are many more who lack style (would you come to a two-star restaurant wearing a cricket sweater,[3] or bicycle clips[4]?), who lack knowledge (one revered critic's last job was on the sports pages!), who are envious of others' success and who are therefore lacking considerably in good judgement.

I think it totally irrelevant to criticize the décor of a restaurant – all such things are personal, and what does it matter anyway? – or

1 Ebury Press, 1994. The dedication reads: "For Mati: also for my daughter Leticia, my son Luciano, and the grandmother they never knew."

2 Has Marco mellowed? Speaking to Bob Mullan, 1998: "Critics are essential. And they are more essential in London than elsewhere. People like A A Gill, Fay Maschler, Jonathan Meades carry tremendous influence. And they've been at it so long that they know what's right and what's wrong. You can't kid them."

3 Reputed to be Matthew Fort, of the *Guardian*.

4 Tom Jaine (they say), then editor of the *Good Food Guide*.

to elaborate for half the review on the designer clothing worn by the restaurant's clientele, male and female. Eating out can be an all-round experience, encompassing surroundings and fellow eaters, but it's the food that matters ultimately. When they home in on all these other things, it really makes me wonder if they can write *at all* about food ...

And their methods of judging chefs and restaurants are, I think, little short of immoral on occasion. A top chef can be hauled over the coals for one less than totally successful dish, because of, say, a wait of a little longer than expected, or for cold bread. Nick Faldo doesn't hit the green every time, Bjorn Borg didn't hit an ace every service game, Sebastian Coe didn't win gold every time he ran, so we are allowed to get it wrong every now and again as well. No top chef is ever going to serve *bad* food, and it certainly could never be so bad that it's worthy of total condemnation. I have to admit that I think food critics in Britain should not, on the whole, be taken seriously.

What had to be taken seriously, above all else, as regards the new venture were the responses of his clientele, many of whom were valued old faithfuls from the days of Harvey's; the verdicts of the inspectors of the *Michelin Guide;* and, not least, the opinion of his partner Rocco Forte.

• • •

If Marco Pierre White had grave misgivings about the value of British food writers, he had no such doubts about the importance, in terms both of prestige and commercial success, of the plump, red *Michelin Guide to Hotels and Restaurants.* Indeed, he was happy to compare the one to the other, to the former's detriment:

The *Guide Michelin*, on the other hand, judges you entirely on what you put on the plate, and on the service. They don't criticize anybody, they don't make facetious comments, they don't run anybody down, they don't tell people how to run their businesses, so it's a guide in the true meaning of the word. When I had long hair, when I was renowned for asking people to leave, when I had a bad press, Michelin were never influenced by that. (Most of my reputation is a product of exaggeration and ignorance anyway.)

I honestly think the most important thing in my career has been the support I've had from Michelin. The French guide has been published every year since 1900; the British one has existed for much less long, but it's now *the* guide to the best restaurants and hotels in the country. Its ratings are regarded as the most objective and impartial, and its judgements are awaited in January every year with bated breath by all of us in the restaurant world.

The Michelin good-food stars are awarded as follows:

A very good restaurant in its category	★
Excellent cooking, worth a detour	★★
Exceptional cuisine, worth a special journey	★★★

The other amenities – such as décor, etc – are measured separately, with the crossed spoon and fork symbol, and range from "plain but good", with one symbol, to "luxury" with five.

Michelin make their awards on the basis of reports from a team of full-time inspectors, as well as letters from the public. The inspectors are recruited from the hotel and restaurant industry, and are highly knowledgeable about every aspect of management, as well as how every classic dish should be prepared. How many food critics can boast that sort of background, and that sort of expertise?

Every listed restaurant is rechecked annually, starred ones more often, and we never know when an inspector will call. He (or she) reserves a table like any other member of the public, without revealing his purpose until after the bill is paid. He then explains who he is and asks to see the kitchen and the cellar. He will report on all the things that any discriminating customer would look for –

the quality of the food, the service, the ambience, the inventiveness of the dishes, the range of the wine list.

At the top level, promotions and demotions are very carefully considered – particularly demotions, since Michelin are well aware of the effect the removal of stars can have on a restaurant's business. I wish food critics would think similarly before letting fly with their unconsidered brickbats.

Many food critics in Britain are actually critical of Michelin. Maybe they object to a foreign tyre company wielding so much power over the restaurant business here, or to its perhaps old-fashioned insistence on continuity and maintaining the highest possible standards. This necessarily precludes them from judging or responding to the new fashions and trends of the moment – the latest restaurant to serve bastardized Italian or sagebrush chicken with sun-dried tomatillos ... I actually think that the food critics here are jealous of Michelin, of the credibility Michelin gets from chefs. The *Guide Michelin* is reliable, objective, and in my opinion has done more for gastronomy in this country than anything or anybody else. I firmly believe that if it weren't for Michelin I wouldn't be where I am today ...

"The tears ran down my face when they told me. It is the highest accolade a chef can ever achieve. There are only 35 restaurants in the world which have three Michelin stars. I have become a member of an elite." – Marco Pierre White, speaking to Lesley Ann Jones in her *News of the World* interview.

In January 1995, Marco was elevated to the *Guide*'s top echelon – the first and still only British chef and, at the age of 33, the youngest chef anywhere ever to be so honoured. Given his views on the importance of Michelin, it is hardly surprising that his first act was, still in tears, to telephone his father (who was then dying of cancer). Sadly, "he didn't understand, really. He knew it was big, but not how big."

The moment, when it came, was not without drama. As he recalled it, years later: "Two men knocked on my door. They told me that in the new *Michelin Guide* about to be published I'd been given three stars. The feeling was amazing, like an athlete winning an Olympic Gold. The difference for me, though, is, unlike an athlete, I can't get away with doing it just once, and people can take it away from me. I have to keep my standards."

A sportsman himself, he seemed to like the sporting analogy. Talking to Bob Mullan for his book of interviews with chefs and restaurateurs, *Off the Menu*, Marco explained:

> In a sense it is the greatest feeling in the world. But you've got to realize it's like being the heavyweight champion of the world. You're not going to keep them for ever, are you? When you get your three stars you no longer have the same hunger. You have to adopt a different strategy. When I won my three stars, I sort of became semi-depressed. I had lost total direction in my life. Because I had achieved what I had set out to achieve. So, you know, "Where do I go from here?" The only way is downhill, isn't it?

As Lynn Barber put it, in the *Observer*, "it was the achievement of his dream, but also its end", a view reinforced by another journalist and friend, who happened to be on the spot on the day of his triumph. Piers Morgan was at The Restaurant, with Michael Winner, hoping to celebrate his achievement with the young maestro himself. Marco, however, as so often at those moments that society likes to mark with speech, presentation and raised glass, had disappeared. (It is not for nothing that a recent TV film about him was entitled by its despairing producers "Waiting for Marco".) It was reported that he had been sighted doing the town with his mentor and now fellow three-star master, Albert Roux. Winner finally tracked him down by telephone and inveigled him back to the Hyde Park Hotel. "I have never seen such euphoria," Morgan says, "but it was euphoria mixed with an enormous sense of anticlimax." There was also, inevitably, regret, as Marco acknowledges – regret that his mother was not there to witness his achievement. "Every boy should build a monument to his mother, it doesn't matter how big or small. I've built that now."

Marco's achievement at The Restaurant was the more remarkable in being double. He had revived a moribund establishment, by his sheer personality turning it into a "destination" restaurant, bringing in a clientele that would not normally frequent such a staid and stately pile as the Hyde Park Hotel. Almost overnight, he had quadrupled turnover. Yet, in arriving at this unprecedented commercial success, to the delight of the hard-headed businessmen who had put their faith in him, he had not sacrificed those high culinary standards that he had set for himself and his loyal team. On the contrary, he had demonstrably raised them, as his elevation to membership of a world elite of chefs by the incorruptible judges of the *Michelin Guide* had proved.

At 33, he was the undisputed first among his peers and crowned with laurels. But White was not the kind of man to rest on them. Could he, his watchful friends demanded, continue at this frenetic pace? Could he, his partners wondered, work the same magic in other unprofitable corners of their empire? Would his financial acuity match his skills as inspirational chef? As Derek Brown, the Michelin chief inspector, noted, others of the elite – Bocuse, the Troisgros brothers, Gagnaire – had lost their way, through dispersal of their talents and energies, over-ambition or financial naïvety.

The young master himself, speaking in 1995, had clearly given the matter some thought: "My best investment has been my name. I intend to build a very large company which will give me an income and allow me to retire at around 40 or 45. My workload is too draining to carry on until I'm 60." Such intellectual clarity, however, might well find itself in the future in conflict with another aspect of his personality, noted by an old friend: "Marco likes a deal." An irresistible one was coming up.

hello
piccadilly

"It was the best deal of my life," Marco told the *Guardian*'s Matthew Fort. "I could retire on what I get from this." "This" was the Criterion, another prime historic site, plumb on Piccadilly Circus, which was, like the Hyde Park Hotel, in the remit of Rocco Forte – as long, that is, as Rocco remained head of the Forte empire, or the empire itself survived.

Times were changing in the London restaurant world. On Valentine's Day, 1993, Terence Conran had opened his first mega-establishment, Quaglino's in Soho, and shown that there was a market for the well-conceived, well-run super-brasserie. Yet the Criterion, a Victorian/Edwardian 200-seater at the whirling hub of London's West End, had not made a profit in 35 years. It had certainly never worked for Forte, even when it was leased to Bob Payton, the energetic American who had made a killing with his Chicago Rib Factory. Could the name and proven talents of Marco Pierre White, now unquestionably the most famous chef in the land, turn a loser into a winner?

"I talked to Marco about it," says Rocco. "We decided the Criterion needed more warmth, and to be moved up-market." David Collins, an architect who specialized in restaurant interiors, was invited to "touch up the décor". Rocco offered Marco 49 per cent of the restaurant (Forte kept 49 per cent and the remaining 2 per cent was held by the landlord, the Sogo group) for nothing. Not surprisingly, Marco agreed. Happily for him, none of these arrangements insisted on his services being exclusive.

Marco had maintained his close friendship with the Lebanese-born Jimmy Lahoud, who had given him a job when he needed one at his restaurant Leoni's Quo Vadis. (Lahoud also owned the celebrated L'Escargot, in Soho.) Together they formed a company, MPW-Criterion, of which Jimmy continues to be operations director, and it has been the vehicle of all Marco's acquisitions, from the Criterion onwards. "The Criterion was the beginning of our business relationship," says Lahoud, "and it has been a great success: our overheads are low, and it has produced fantastic figures." For such a relationship to endure, of course, total trust between the partners would seem a fundamental necessity. That it exists in this case seems well established by an interview given by Lahoud to Lynn Barber of the *Observer*: "Marco is unbelievably kind and trusting. I called him one day and told him a deal I was doing had fallen through and could he lend me half a million. He said, 'Cash or cheque?' and biked a cheque around that afternoon."

With his developing interest in art and decoration, and his growing awareness of the importance of "front of house" in the restaurant business, the restoration of the Criterion was an agreeable challenge for Marco. This "fabulous room", as one journalist described it, was "an Edwardian vision of a Turkish seraglio on the same scale as Liverpool Street Station. God knows what it would cost to create now."

Like the renewed lighting, the restoration was discreet. The room's Orientalist paintings – far from being examples of great art, but deeply evocative for those visitors who had such works and other trophies of Empire in their homes – were put back in place, the golden-mosaic ceiling retouched and the harem-style drapery refreshed. (The customer, acclimatized after a pleasant hour or two in this exotic place, is staggered on emerging by the time warp of the backpack hordes eating hamburgers at the sooty foot of the statue of Eros, usually in the rain.)

This being, after all, a restaurant, the usual close attention was paid to the food. Loyal troops, trained in the Marco tradition, were brought into the kitchen from The Restaurant (Peter Reffell and Roger Pizey leading them). A sophisticated but affordable menu was designed (with a line-drawing of the young master modestly decorating its cover), and outside, a discreet plaque bore the new name of the establishment (making good use of the new *patron's* "best investment"): "The Criterion Brasserie – Marco Pierre White". The power of the strange, trilingual name had once before not only summoned the faithful but alerted strangers to interesting developments. Could it do the same trick in another place and for another market?

"When Marco Pierre White told me he was taking over the Criterion, I said, 'Ridiculous! You can't park, you have to walk through those night-time oddities that hang around Eros to get there …' Needless to say, Marco ignored my advice, opened up, and has done splendidly." A chastened Michael Winner, writing in the *Sunday Times* in his bluff, just-a-fellow-punter way (having, as any sensible chap would do, left his chauffeur with the Rolls parked on a taxi rank nearby), was nevertheless not impressed by the restaurant's recent makeover. "People always say the Criterion is such a lovely room. I think it looks like a Victorian gents' toilet. That still places it well above the visual standard of most new restaurants." He didn't much like the clientele either – "looked to me like the public you see on quiz shows" – but the aspect later improved: "Various upper-class shoppers had arrived with carrier bags." As for the food, the ballotine of salmon was very good, though "the bread was awful". The haddock was excellent too, but the fried skate "dodgy". That, though, was made up for by a side order of chicken consommé that was "lovely". Rounding out the meal, and no doubt the figure, "I finished with two jellies – red fruit and Sauternes – and I had a bit of treacle tart. All superb." Winner's somewhat grudging conclusion: "I'm not surprised Marco made it work, really. And if you're addicted to gold mosaic ceilings and Victorian Arab décor, you could even find it wondrous."

Writing some time after the opening in October 1995, Lucy

Humphries of the restaurant guide *Square Meal* praised the "first-class French brasserie food" in "this huge exotic Ottoman fantasy". Perhaps feeling challenged by such abandoned delving in the vocabulary, Fay Maschler in the London *Evening Standard* fought back with: "Byzantine splendour now bewitchingly lit by designer David Collins* who has also added swathes of fabric which bring to mind the school of Orientalism in French painting." Acknowledging that the new proprietor had been fortunate in his surroundings, Maschler added that "White has also been savvy in installing a populous brigade of formally dressed waiting staff, the majority of them French. It reinforces the notion that within this shimmering 19th century interior you are somewhere far away from the panhandlers of 20th century Leicester Square." Noting that the chefs here came from The Canteen, Maschler presciently observed that "this is not a brasserie menu in terms of the hours in which it is served nor, truly, in essence. The cooking is too sophisticated. Marco knows no other way, a 'failing' which should and will draw the crowds." Among the dishes on offer, the "delectability of fillet of smoked haddock [an import from The Canteen] with poached egg, new potatoes and grain mustard beurre blanc" brought out the best, or perhaps the worst, in Maschler's prose style: "The curvaceous, opalescent divisions of lightly smoked – indubitably low-tar – fish contrasting with bland potatoes, smarmy soft egg yolk and the bite of mustard is the perfect brasserie dish."

Matthew Fort in the *Guardian*, revisiting "as splendid an interior in which to eat as anywhere in the world", was pleased that "the exoticism has been carefully cherished and enhanced by clever lighting and pastiche paintings". However, he had his doubts about "the swag of paradise-blue chiffon curtaining that acts as a coy partition between the bar and the dining room". As for the food, "In the past I have had the odd word of misgiving about the kind of tucker Marco Pierre White puts out. I am now happy to eat humble pie, as long as MPW

---

* Marco's longtime collaborator, currently suffering, or enjoying, one of those "gap years" that seem inevitable in such relationships.

has prepared the recipe. Of course, he does not cook at the Criterion. He is too busy elsewhere. But he causes the food to be cooked. He plots the menu, he trains the brigade, he sees that everything is tickety-boo." And everything, he affirms, *was* tickety-boo: "When I dream of the tarte Bordelue with crisp, buttery pastry, fragrant poached pears and perfumed almond filling, I wake up smiling."

The ever-faithful Emily Green, writing in the *Independent* under the heavy-breathing headline, "The love shack: Marco Pierre White's voluptuous new venue", found the "long, vaulted, mirrored room, lamplight glowing against the gilded ceiling" of this 121-year-old, listed building more reminiscent of "the neo-baroque excesses of 1870 Budapest than brick and stucco London, but in London it is, bang on the south side of Piccadilly, lurking behind a pavement populated by beggars and buskers and an unpromising frontage". With the help of the designer David Collins, White, "who has had enough girlfriends

---

fish tales

When we arrived back at the Hyde Park Hotel after a second fishing trip, a staff member brought White several new hand-built Bruce and Walker Hexagraph rods that had been delivered in our absence. One by one, he unlaced the red-velvet cases and slid out the shining sections of rod, examining them minutely.

"How many of those rods have you got now, Marco?" one of the waiters asked.

"Fifty-five," White replied.

"All exactly the same?" the waiter asked.

"All exactly the same," White said.

The waiter persisted with his questions. "So why do you go on buying them, then?"

White squinted along one of the rod sections, checking the alignment of the rings, and then returned it carefully to its case.

"Because I can," he said.

– **Luke Jennings, the *New Yorker***

---

and wives to know a romantic restaurant when he sees one", had "created a room that is the architectural equivalent of a love potion". Recovering her poise, Emily Green added, "By the way, the food is good, too." And the wine list was "full of peachy bottles".

The impressionable Green would have been jealous of her colleague Helen Fielding, of the *Independent on Sunday*. Having ordered a cigar and finding that it cost more than her main course, she pointed this out to the great chef himself, conveniently seated alone at the next table. "Far from throwing us out, Marco murmured in Mr Darcy-like tones, full of repressed emotions, 'You have made a valid point. Can I reimburse you for your cigar?'"

Whether or not the varied views of the critics had an impact on the public's perception of Marco's repackaged Criterion, it soon began to look as if his judgement of the potential was to prove accurate. "Very quickly, people started to come in," Rocco Forte remembers. "Gross turnover was soon up to £4 million a year." (Today the figure is put at around £7 million, with a reported profit of £2 million annually.) "A very successful venture indeed."

Marco now had money, staff to deploy (or be lost to competitors) and a head full of concepts. Rocco was, understandably, eager to help him achieve his aims. Patrick Copeland, a businessman with long experience of the "hospitality" arm of the hotel and entertainment industry, joined Forte around the time of the Criterion launch. Long before meeting Marco, he had followed his career, dining at Harvey's and The Canteen. "Rocco put him on the right path," says Copeland. "The Hyde Park was where Marco went from being a chef to becoming a businessman. Before that – at The Canteen, for example – he was engaged in making someone else's concepts work. At The Restaurant, he was flying solo, and he made it work. But the real Marco emerged when Rocco put him into the Criterion: he made it work even better." With Copeland, Marco travelled the country, looking at Forte properties in need of resuscitation. (They often flew, belying Marco's declared fear of flying, a factor in his insularity. "Small planes are different" is his explanation.) "For every establishment, he had an idea, a concept, almost immediately. He's a student of his business, he is intuitive, he has an encyclopedic memory and he can produce a variety of ideas for making something work." For Copeland, the image of Marco as a brash, wild man was "a carefully cultivated gimmick, which he would now like not to have, because he knows it's not him. I see the contrary – a loving person."

Rocco, naturally keen to see Marco work his wonders on other places, talked about the Palm Court – a relic of another way of life – at the Waldorf, and of a possible move of The Restaurant into the Meridien Hotel in Piccadilly. The latter, a stone's throw from the Criterion, would be within the empire-within-an-empire that Marco, with his partner Jimmy Lahoud, was carefully creating in the West End. Empires, however, notoriously fall, and the Forte empire, as was about to be demonstrated, was no exception to the rule.

In November 1995, a month after the opening of the Criterion, Granada, the media conglomerate – and, with 45,000 rooms, the UK's biggest hotelier – launched a hostile takeover bid against the Forte empire. In January of the following year, Rocco Forte was forced to capitulate and Marco, while continuing to explore ways of expanding his own fief, entered into negotiations with Charles Allen, the Granada chief executive. The potential advantages of a collaboration between the country's top hotelier and its star chef seemed manifestly clear to both parties. As the *New Yorker* racily phrased it, "Granada's hospitality division was best known for the catering at its motorway rest stops, and it badly needed a touch of culinary glamour, whereas White, by then hell-bent on expansion, needed more properties."

The canny Matthew Fort, a seasoned Marco-watcher, pointed out in the *Guardian*, "Granada may have inherited the [Forte] deal, but, not unnaturally, given the awesome profitability of the Criterion since White's involvement, they are very keen to keep him sweet, so keen that they have bought up the outstanding two per cent of shares, and given one to him." As for Marco's own activities (in cooperation with his partner Jimmy Lahoud), Fort commented, "The last 18 months have seen an extraordinary explosion in Marco Pierre White's acquisitions. First, it was the joint venture with Rocco Forte to bring new life to one of London's most remarkable and striking restaurant sites, the Criterion in Piccadilly. Then he bought Les Saveurs in Curzon Street, then its next-door neighbour, the antique Mirabelle. The latest project to hit the headlines has been the joint venture with Damien Hirst to relaunch the venerable Quo Vadis."

Marco's financial acuity (which cannot have gone unnoticed by the Scottish-born Charles Allen) brought further praise from the *Guardian's* man: "While the Criterion may be the finest bargain so far, other parts of the growing White empire have been picked up for extraordinarily little money. Les Saveurs, a restaurant with a substantial reputation, he bought for a reputed £200,000 and the Mirabelle for £1.5 million. If these prices seem extravagant, it needs to be pointed out that you should budget something around £1–£1.5 million [at 1996 rates] if you're planning to set up a 70- to 80-cover restaurant in central London."

Underlining Marco's eye for top quality at bargain prices, Fort points out that "to pick up prime sites for those sums makes them a snip, particularly when the cellar [alone] at Les Saveurs has been valued at half the cost price [of the restaurant] and when the yearly rent on the Mirabelle is a paltry £1,000 a year". According to Fort, "White says he has already been offered £1 million over what he paid for the 37-year lease."

• • •

These sums pale to nothing when the potential of the Granada/Marco deal is scrutinized, as it was by the practised eye of the *Financial Times.* Its contributor, Nicholas Lander, who has personal experience of the restaurant scene, noted that "once established, the joint venture will roll out and incorporate up to 200 hotel dining rooms around the UK. The five-year plan projects eventual sales of £50 million, generating profits of 15–20 per cent net – double the industry norm and serving 2 million customers annually, as many as pass through the portals of Conran restaurants."

For Charles Allen, following Rocco Forte, the problem of hotel dining rooms, which hitherto had been only "reasonably profitable", could now be addressed. Not only would it increase the return to Granada shareholders but there would also be the bonus that "busy restaurants will attract more people into our hotels". For Marco, the future could only seem bright. His friend Michael Winner recently expressed fears for him "now that he is an employee", a view countered by Rocco Forte, speaking (perhaps a trifle ruefully) today in the boardroom of his newly formed company, RF Hotels. "Marco doesn't act like an employee, he thinks and acts like a principal. He has 50 per cent, so he can't be thrown out, and if he was, the [Granada] restaurants would fail. And he has been given a line of investment into all those restaurants: he doesn't have to use his own money."

• • •

"Tonight's menu: cow's brains in formaldehyde, followed by pickled sheep served with a sneer." This was the fare confidently promised to her readers by Catherine Milner in the *Sunday Telegraph* of 4th August 1996, when "London's angriest duo" opened a new restaurant in Soho. Karl Marx had lived in rooms above it and, since 1926, when it opened its doors as Soho's first Italian restaurant, many a cow and sheep had been consumed there, but none, so far, had been displayed in a suspension of formaldehyde. That, however, was a distinct possibility – or so the buzz went – when the Turner Prize-winning artist Damien Hirst and Marco Pierre White (along with a Freud and a Kennedy) took over the ancient institution in Dean Street then known as Leoni's Quo Vadis.

Not only, coincidentally, was Hirst, like Marco, a Yorkshire lad from Leeds, but they had also attended the same school, although Hirst was in a superior class, with one of Marco's older brothers. Marco's partner, Jimmy Lahoud, owned the old restaurant, with its peeling, olive-green exterior, sporting a blue plaque recording that Marx had lived there, and Italian tricolor flags. Within, there were the starched traditional tablecloths and those tired-looking elderly waiters in greening tail coats, and the equally tired-looking *hors d'oeuvre* trolleys that were inseparable from the traditional Soho dining experience.

The success of such nearby monster modern eateries as Conran's made-over Quaglino's and the more recent Mezzo – "eating palaces for the well-heeled masses", in one journalist's description – had sounded the death-knell of places like Leoni's Quo Vadis. Lahoud, of course, had first met Marco here, when the chef had come, in pre-Harvey days, to regroup and replenish his coffers. He knew, from the Hyde Park and the Criterion, what his partner could do to bring new life – and big crowds – to moribund institutions. For Marco, it was another challenge, and challenges were, so to speak, meat and drink to him. (And who else would have had the quirky panache to replace the Soho-Italian cuisine with his own French classical while replacing the Italian flags with the Union Jack?)

> **vignette**
> He remembers my wife's name and what she does for a living. I can see myself working for him for many, many years to come.
> – **Philip Cooper, head chef, Quo Vadis**

The other partners in the enterprise, with Hirst, were Matthew Freud,* conveniently head of a thriving public relations firm, and Jonathan Kennedy, a marketing man and friend of Marco's from the days of Harvey's. (These three, later bought out by Marco, went on to create Pharmacy in Notting Hill Gate.)

"You don't see Marco in other restaurants or at social gatherings," his new partner Kennedy points out. "On the other hand, he spends a vast amount of time in his own restaurants. His attention to detail is extraordinary. Marco is at his best when he is sitting in a restaurant looking at everything going on around him. Marco is a one-off – a very extraordinary man. He does fall out dramatically with people – but that's a by-product of the sheer intensity of his life." His partnership with Jimmy Lahoud, Kennedy says, "works brilliantly: Marco fills the restaurants, Jimmy makes sure they make money".

A sum reputed to be £2 million was to be spent on the refurbishment of Quo Vadis, with Hirst responsible for selecting the furniture and colour scheme. Upstairs there would be a bar, cheerfully decorated with surgical instruments in display cases; the ground floor would be a combination of dining room and gallery. There was talk of pickled shark and stuffed bear: whether as display or on the menu was not clear. Hirst, it was said, would pocket ten per cent of the takings.

As with all of Marco's ventures to date, when Quo Vadis reopened, in January 1999, the people came. As Lucy Humphries of the restaurant guide *Square Meal* put it, the new Quo Vadis was "notorious for Damien Hirst but admirable chiefly for its very precise cooking". The clientele had changed too: "Soho's finest ad-men in Armani suits, magazine editors in short skirts and stilettos, and film

* Matthew Freud was no slouch (as they say in such circles) as a PR man, and the well-publicized choice of flayed cows' heads in tanks of formaldehyde as appropriate décor for a restaurant had ensured a stormy opening for the repackaged Quo Vadis. There were noisy demonstrations by animal liberationists, staff members were threatened, the police were called and five arrests were made. Marco recalls that, as he looked down from the bar at the demonstrators in the street below on a cold January night, "I was thinking of sending the boys out with hot coffee for them. I couldn't have asked for better publicity."

people in designer shirts and leather jackets. Boring Surrey-man will not feel at home here," advised Humphries. Marco put one of his brightest chefs, Philip Cooper, in charge of the kitchen and Michelin awarded a star – curiously, a rarity in this restaurant-rich sector of London – for his cooking.

As ever, the critics came too, and, as ever in England, editors reached for their best card-carrying comedians. Under the predictable headline "Sea Scallops in Formaldehyde", the late John Wells, reporting for the *Independent on Sunday*, noted that the participation of "famous charcutier Damien Hirst" was "unspecified". His companions "were already mourning the old restaurant before we got through the door. They remembered it when it was old Soho Italian, Leoni's Quo Vadis, offering spaghetti followed by veal, when Signor Leoni himself used to wander from table to table rather lugubriously talking about Positano – and it wasn't at all expensive." Regretting that "the spit-roast suckling pig was off, possibly on loan to another exhibition", Wells was pleased to see "some good solid Damien Hirst animal pieces like calf's liver, grilled ribeye, roast rabbit, lamb, duck and chicken". However, he eschewed informed criticism in favour of limp attempts at humour: "Our guests were not wild about the salmon, thinking it was farmed."

The *Sunday Times*, in its wisdom, chose a barrister turned TV chat-show host to cover the art and cuisine. With becoming, if justified, modesty, Clive Anderson confessed, "I was worried about my qualifications for the task ahead. I do work in Soho, but I am more familiar with its sandwich bars." However, "Quo Vadis is now in the hands of Marco Pierre White, so I can claim some background knowledge. One lunchtime, in connection with my television show, I met him at The Restaurant at the Hyde Park Hotel. Although he enjoys the reputation of being one of the rudest men in catering, to me he seemed perfectly amiable. Was he losing his touch, or am I? He elaborated on the bewildering array of financial, legal and culinary deals he was doing until I abandoned all thought of actually eating. But getting on for teatime, he drifted back to the kitchen and produced a meal that was simply stunning. So could Quo Vadis match up to this?" Answering his own question, Anderson found that "by Soho standards the premises of Quo Vadis are large, without straying into the canteen proportions of Mezzo". The place had been "elegantly refurbished in a minimalist style: off-yellow floors with off-white lighting". Was the cabinet of anatomical instruments an original Hirst or "a first-aid kit now required by EU regulations"? Nevertheless, "the idea of art in a restaurant is inspired, as the two worlds match each other for glamour and pretension". Anderson reported that "service throughout was attentive to the point of perfection" and, as for the food, "although the cooking did not reach the heights of Marco HQ, this was definitely somewhere for a good night out".

Declining, unlike its rivals, to send in the clowns, the *Daily Telegraph* elected instead to assign a millionaire composer of musical comedies to the task of restaurant criticism. With great good fortune, or incredible prescience, Andrew Lloyd Webber happened to have on his library shelves a copy of a book jauntily entitled *I Shall Die on the Carpet*, the autobiography, published in 1966, of one Peppino Leoni, restaurateur and founder of Quo Vadis. "Armed with a slice of the low-down on this venerable site," confided the composer, mixing his metaphors with impunity, "a visit seemed in order."

"The décor is bog-standard, late-nineties mega-restaurant," Lloyd Webber decided. "If old Peppino Leoni were alive he would have to retitle the book *I Shall Die on the Varnished Stripped Pine*." Apart from an unfortunate episode when an ill-clamped snail shot across the restaurant, leaving the composer somewhat discomposed, things went well. The remaining molluscs constituted "an old-fashioned perfectly executed dish", the chicken liver parfait "was pronounced by my guest the best he had ever tasted" and "the calves' liver with bacon and sage could not be faulted". Indeed, "everything the chef cooked seemed thought through and perfectly balanced".

Ben Rogers (not a known comic or composer: could he be a food critic?) of the *Independent* also invoked the good Peppino, claiming to have had "the very last lunch ever eaten at the old Leoni's Quo Vadis". The food there, however, "had never been authentic. Prawn cocktail could be followed by sirloin flamed in whisky ... I imagined the new [restaurant] would be, by contrast, brash and loud. But I was wrong. It's true the dessert trolleys and the flambé equipment have gone (will they ever again be seen in a fashionable London restaurant?) but the new ground-floor dining room is quiet and elegant. Leoni, you feel, would have approved." The clientele rivalled the room: "Every other man in the place seemed to be in a Savile Row suit." And although it was "strange to see all this bad-boy art nestled in such cosy surroundings ... the effect was incongruous and rather sweet". The meal itself "fairly sparkled". Rogers added, "The cooking is fancier than at the nearby Criterion but in the same modern French style, and the menu features some trusted *new* favourites – parfait of foie gras and chicken livers, for instance, and lemon tart, all, doubtless, with their customary zing." The truffle vinaigrette on the asparagus was pronounced "melodious" (perhaps he is a composer after all) and the haddock with poached egg "faultless". All in all, "I suspect that Leoni's is going to remain more congenial than Soho's other mega-restaurants. A worthy successor to the old place, it's got class, and should run and run."

More than two years later, Quo Vadis is indeed still running, and retains its Michelin star. Changes, however, are in view, now that Marco has assumed sole ownership. He has never been happy with the look of Quo Vadis. There'll certainly be some changes made: one can only hope Peppino would have approved.

• • •

By contrast with the Soho establishment, another property, MPW, in the new business project of Canary Wharf, seems to have been acquired in a quiet moment of distraction. "Marco thought it looked pretty," Jimmy Lahoud said. Renamed Big Chef by Marco (a tongue-in-cheek salute to the distinctly down-market Little Chef chain of eateries owned by his new partners, Granada), it is a brasserie serving the kind of classy but affordable food that contributed to the popularity of the Criterion. Set in a shopping mall, at the top of an escalator, it is a haven of quality and good taste but somehow – partly because of its far-flung location in east London – remains outside the (mainly West End) Marco Pierre White portfolio.

The West End, and especially that choice part of it called Mayfair, is where the action now was. The question of moving Marco's flagship restaurant out of the Hyde Park Hotel and into the Meridien Hotel on Piccadilly had already been mooted in discussions between Marco and Rocco Forte. Granada, the new owners of both properties, saw the advantages of such a transfer, particularly in view of a long-term plan to weed out for sale the less profitable elements of their acquisition – of which the Hyde Park was one. Marco, as always, had his reasons too.

Of the Oak Room in the Meridien, Lucy Humphries observed in her *Square Meal* profile, "Marco had had his eye on this room for some years. As a custodian of Michelin values, he knows this is a proper setting for his skills, and [cunningly anticipating the line taken by future critics] make no mistake about it, he is still very much a working chef. This is a kitchen-led company." For Granada, the attractions were just as obvious (and, as Nicholas Lander pointed out in the *Financial Times,* "such arrangements only flourish when both sides feel they are getting an equal share of the spoils"). As has been noted, hotel dining rooms everywhere were under-performing, abandoned by hotel guests seeking the attraction of more glamorous restaurants. "The Oak Room, for example," Lander reported, "was taking only £8,000 a week before White moved in, but it is anticipated that this will soon rise to £40,000."

Marco's motivations for the move were more complex – and, as usual, more concerned with the emotions:

> When I won my three stars, I sort of became semi-depressed. I had
> lost total direction in my life, because I had achieved what I set out
> to achieve. So, you know, "Where do I go from here?" The only

way is downhill, isn't it? So once I pulled myself out of the doom and gloom … I put all my energies into the front of house, as a result of which we now have the greatest dining room in Britain. We're the only restaurant in Britain with five red knives and forks [in the *Michelin Guide*], which represent the ultimate in service, the ultimate dining room.

Quite apart from its usefulness in filling an emotional need and its convenient location within sprinting distance (for the former running champ) of the rest of Marco's rapidly expanding mini-empire in the heart of the capital, the Oak Room had, in the eyes of both parties to the deal, a longer-term significance. "How can you keep three stars [never mind all that crimson cutlery] and expand like this?" asked Lucy Humphries of *Square Meal*. She answered her own question thus: "Think Saint Laurent, think Karl Lagerfeld. Couture line plus ready-to-wear and a host of diffusion ranges which carry the message into different price levels without diminishing the sure touch of the master." There, in that last phrase, is the rub.

There is nothing new in the commercial exercise known as branding. It has even been practised in the restaurant business, notably by Terence Conran, a natural enough development for a retailer. But it has never been attempted on the scale envisaged by the partnership. The joint venture, once established, would roll out and incorporate some 200 hotel dining rooms around the UK. A five-year plan projected eventual sales of £50 million, generating profits of 15–20 per cent net: double the industry norm and serving two million customers annually, as many as pass through the portals of Conran restaurants. More problematic than the scale of the operation, though, was the fact that the protagonist was a chef, and no chef in the history of cuisine had ever attempted such a feat.

(There is, however, an Awful Warning in the catastrophe that followed the acquisition of another great restaurant by, as it happened, another master – but in this case a master of couture. When, in 1981, Pierre Cardin bought the historic Parisian restaurant

Maxim's – three Michelin stars, five red knives and forks and all – he proceeded on a classic exercise in branding. Not only did he open a Maxim's at Paris's Orly airport and others in such far-flung and unlikely places as Beijing and Singapore, but he also launched a range of packaged goods bearing the sacred name. An immediate result was the removal by a horrified Michelin of all the stars and knives and forks, followed shortly afterwards by the complete removal from the *Guide* of the original hallowed institution itself.)

The first task for Marco, however, before the branding exercise could start, was to get the flagship up and sailing. "I believe the most important ingredient in a restaurant," the chef-turned-front-of-house-enthusiast declared, "is the creation of an environment which people want to immerse themselves in … it forces them to spend money." Waving a massive hand at the vast space of the Oak Room, Marco helpfully explained, "Now when you walk in *here* the first thing you are mesmerized by is the beauty of the room, the chandelier, the sheer opulence of the room. You're taken aback before you've actually eaten anything. Once you're inside these doors, you're no longer in the Meridien Hotel."

Support for Marco's claims, although in more measured terms, is supplied by Luke Jennings in the *New Yorker*:

> The hotel lobby, with its canned music and club-class ambience, gives no clue to the considered luxuries that lie behind the Oak Room's mirrored doors. He has transformed the Oak Room – previously little more than a tourist dining room – into London's grandest and most expensive restaurant. The room's oppressive décor, with its giltwork and massive chandeliers, has been neutralized by art works from White's collection and, most particularly, by his Bugatti bronzes of jungle animals which, shining and muscular, pace eye-level plinths.

The artist Richard Bramble, in his painterly book, *The Star Chefs Cookbook*, elaborates on this:

Marco's current treasure at the Oak Room is a wonderful collection of animal bronzes, the work of sculptor Rembrandt Bugatti (1885–1916), brother of the more famous Ettore, the man behind the classic motor-car marque. Though rare, there are quite a few bronzes, including an elephant, lion, lioness and hippopotamus. I could tell how much Marco cared for them when one morning he excitedly showed me and everyone else present the new moose he had bought. Marco is also particularly fond of a series of 18th-century kitchen and chef paintings by Ribor and is always on the lookout for more.

Significantly, in view of the obvious question critics would be asking about the changed priorities of the reconstructed star chef, Bramble, who spent four months doing a water-colour of the interior, has this to say: "Despite the success and media attention, he insists he is still learning and has yet to achieve his potential. For this reason it is rare for Marco not to be in the kitchen during a service, though with his growing list of restaurants, unless he has become a mystic, he cannot be in more than one place at once." This, clearly, would be a loss, since, as the painter observed, "Watching Marco cook is a unique experience, as he prepares the food as if always for the first and last time, with total fascination, concentration and care."

Reassuringly for his faithful supporters, Luke Jennings confirmed that "cooking may have made White a rich man, but he is still addicted to the theatre of his trade". Jennings had the rare privilege, one night, of seeing him perform:

As the tables filled, the backstage tension built. Dishes are assembled in stages and dressed at a final inspection station known as the *passe,* from which they are delivered on trays to the customers. As both quality controller and working chef, White moves at speed between the *passe* and his workstation. That night, he was handling fish. He brought intense concentration to each brief act of cooking, laying the soft fillets of mullet and brill in the hissing cast-iron pans, finger tasting the sabayon and the jus niçoise, hurrying the vegetables around their skillets, and, finally, with all the elements achieving critical perfection at the same moment, dressing the plates. Around him, as orders were bellowed from the *passe* ("One trotter, one rouget, one St Pierre, *et vite!*"), others were duplicating White's choreography, though none quite managed his speed. The activity, at its loudest and most urgent, seemed to bring him a kind of peace.

The customers came, as they had before, although they were not the same kind of people. The idea informing his other new restaurants may have been, in Marco's coining, "affordable glamour"; at £40 a head they attracted not the old expense-account pinstripe set but (in Jennings's phrase), "the demotic-speaking meritocrats of fashion, sport and the media" – the fauna of Blairite New Labour. But the huge space and elevated prices of the Oak Room drew a different, more affluent crowd. On another visit, this time to the front of house, Jennings "recognized a model and one of London's more nubile heiresses, but for the most part, the clientele evinced a dark-suited anonymity". As for the cost, and the profitability, he had this to say:

> The Oak Room is regarded by White as his couture line, and, as such, is freed from any requirement to be profitable. All is sacrificed to sensation, and I left the restaurant as I suspect many leave it: slowly, and in a state of almost post-coital bemusement. The bill [for four] came to £580, which by then seemed normal – sensible, even. White rang me the next morning. "We mugged you," he explained. "But we mugged you without violence."

The critics came too. Understandably, the *Daily Telegraph* assigned its resident multimillionaire to the job. In the time-honoured tradition of British restaurant critics, Andrew Lloyd Webber devoted the first six paragraphs to the history and architecture of the Piccadilly Hotel (as it then was) and to reminiscences about tea taken there on Sunday afternoons with his father, who went for the music of the five-piece orchestra, alas reduced to three. "This, in his view, was the beginning of the end. Soon there'd be only a pianist. Next there'd be no music at all. Dad was right, of course. Very soon these events transpired. Now there is Marco Pierre White."

Still in nostalgic vein, he continued, "I don't know what my father would make of the Oak Room at the Piccadilly Hotel, rather Le Meridien, today. I don't know whether its irascible genius of a chef would drive him into a rare rage or have him hiding under the table quivering with terror." Lloyd Webber nevertheless sat down, with, as he claimed, an open mind, in "the vast, windowless, oak-lined, chandelier-bedecked Edwardian room that is now his shrine".

"I must report," wrote the fair-minded composer, "that food of a quality you rarely encounter emerged, albeit lengthily, with the effortless sure handling ascribed to a Mercedes." Regrettably for his readers, who might have hoped for something more specific, he concluded, "Really there's not a lot of point in dissecting dishes, for they're all superb and the ingredients are all top-notch." He did, however, make an exception for the mashed potatoes, which "looked and tasted like edible velvet" and "the famous pig's trotter", which lived up to its reputation.

On a second visit (it was, after all, as Lloyd Webber explained, "the only restaurant that has earned a 10 out of 10 from a clear majority of foodies") his companion was "the ever-lustrous Sir John Mills". Disastrously, "he wanted something plain. I winced. What would be the reaction of the head waiter? No restaurant could have been more accommodating. He chose turbot, which the kitchen plainly grilled, and they even made him a special *amuse-gueule* of asparagus rather than the scallops we were offered." All in all, "expensive it may be, but I cannot wait to return".

Sophie Grigson, foodie daughter of the foodie icon Jane Grigson, sailed bravely in for the *Independent on Sunday:* "Well, shiver my timbers, it certainly is a stunning setting. Marco is probably right when he says it is the grandest and most beautiful dining room in

London. The pale oak-panelled walls rise majestically up to the lofty ceiling, with a touch of gold here and there, and vast mirrors. As you walk into the room, the sheer scale of it quite takes your breath away. Yet despite this grandeur, it isn't an intimidating room, or even an impersonal one."

Recovering her breath, Sophie cased the joint and spotted "a large group of advertising execs" – well, "the 40ish guy with flowing locks and snappy suit was a dead giveaway" – and a young couple, "possibly a rock star and his partner with oodles of dosh". Happily, though, "you don't have to be incredibly wealthy to eat here. At lunchtime, there is a fabulously tempting menu which begins with oysters in a champagne jelly, as far as I can recall, for a mere £29.50", which you can enjoy "while the delightful waiters cosset you into a state of blissful serenity".

Thus armed with a dubious memory and a girlish prose-style, Sophie was saved in the nick of time from the stress of making grown-up decisions: "As it happens, we went for the full Monty, largely due to the boss." (The man *does* seem to have a mystic ability to be everywhere at once.) "Part of Marco's charm is his unabashed delight in his work and success. Like a little boy with a new toy, he is chuffed to pieces to be in the Oak Room … his grin spreads from ear to ear. The other part of his charm is that he cooks like an angel. And when such an angel offers to manage your lunch for you, who could possibly refuse?"

Not our Sophie: "The £75 à la carte meal arrived, course after heavenly course" until: "I was kind of hoping that the mini-breast of a crème caramel trembling before us was the last offering. It was lovely, with its jaunty little raisin poised on top." Post-prandial readers of the Sunday Indy who were still awake were finally rewarded by some thoughtful observations. "When the glow and the glamour were receding, I realized that I had been utterly seduced by a meal that had very little connection with the 'modern British' eclectic school of cooking. No bandwagoning here. No East meets West, no char-grilling, no sun-dried tomatoes, no caper berries, no trendy ingredients for trend's sake." Here was "a blessed, rare oasis in the desert of anything goes".

Among the milder of Marco's published strictures on the quality and performance of British restaurant critics is this: "I don't think anyone who runs sausage-cooking competitions in a newspaper should be allowed within a mile of a top-class restaurant." It was not enough, however, to prevent Matthew Fort (for he was the object of Marco's disaffection), stalwart of the *Guardian,* from breaching the mirrored portals of the Oak Room: "the flagship, the standard bearer, landmark and benchmark, hushed, plushed and expensive to know. The grandest dining room with the best original works of art, the most expensive menu, a wine list of mythological proportions and prices, suavity of service, opulence of appeal."

Fort, a close and knowledgeable observer of the rise and rise of the lad from Leeds, noted, "There were a few mutterings when M P W moved his top-notch operation from one end of Piccadilly (Hyde Park Hotel) to the other without a twitch to his three Michelin stars, but the new place was distinctly more majestic, and the menu, polish and performance were undimmed." Visiting in the first week of operation ("scarcely a fair time to test a kitchen *brigade* that is still settling into its new playground – although, it must be said, there was no similar period of grace as far as the bill was concerned"), Fort found faults, but also merit: "Each dish is brilliantly orchestrated for both the eye and the mouth." Invoking once again the dichotomy between the British critics' and the chefs' views of the *Michelin Guide,* Fort concludes, "There is no doubt that this is a great dining experience, although, in my view, the cooking lacks the brilliant edge it had in the heady days of Harvey's. I think that the chef's holy grail of three Michelin stars is as much about consistency as it is about the originality of the food." Fortunately, "subsequent reports suggest that the early flaws have been ironed out".

The move from one end of Piccadilly to the other had a marked effect on the majestic Jonathan Meades of *The Times,* another long-time observer (and friend, but then so are all the London critics).

Having given Marco a heady score of 9 out of 10 at the Hyde Park, he had elevated him, after a second visit, to a vertiginous 10 out of 10. In doing so, Meades could not resist a swipe at Michelin and its own rather more ancient scoring system. Regretting, like Fort, the loss of the "off-the-wall" cooking at Harvey's, forsaken in the drive for Michelin recognition ("which means rehearsed cooking and stiff service to city yobs and rock stars"), Meades nevertheless conceded that the gaining of three stars – by "the first native Briton and the youngest chef anywhere" – was "a considerable achievement".

Following Marco to the Meridien, Meades makes "no apology for writing about Marco Pierre White for the second time in as many months: he is the dominant chef of the age and, beyond that, its leading luxury restaurateur" (a neat encapsulation of Marco's unique culinary status). "The Oak Room in the Meridien is the *ne plus ultra* of Edwardian baroque interiors … a vast space, the size of about four squash courts. Although they enjoy no natural light, the rooms are far from oppressive – and who needs natural light when there are six chandeliers like a Brobdingnagian's missus's earrings, the same fellow's shaving mirrors, each of them 20 feet tall, and a ceiling that's twice that height?"

As for the food: "The right note is struck over and again. There is no resort to embellishment; there is total trust in integration, fine ingredients, spot-on timing, perfect balance, lightness of touch." Marco's dishes here "draw … on the canon of old and grand French classicism. And to the most wonderful, most pleasurable, most eye-opening effect. This is the cream of Escoffier, this is the distillate of *Larousse Gastronomique*, this is currently the best luxury cooking in Britain." Not surprisingly, in view of this paean of praise, as he controversially had with his Michelin stars, the translated Marco retained his Meades award of 10 out of 10.

Whether or not, as these two "middle-weight" reviewers (Marco's assessment – there are no heavyweights) suggest, some youthful culinary verve has been lost on the hard road from Harvey's, there may, understandably, have been some loss of speed. Marco recently recalled, "I was running through Harvey's one day – I used to run everywhere then – and Oliver Reed [the famously pugilistic film actor] got up from his table and ran after me. I stopped and said, 'What are you running for?' And he stopped too and said, 'Where's the fight?'"

Cooks' tour

The chefs quoted below are among the 85 or so friends, employees, colleagues and relatives who responded – usually eagerly – to invitations to talk to the author about the subject of this book. No doubt for excellent reasons of their own, all the distinguished chefs who were White's mentors – Albert Roux, Pierre Koffmann, Nico Ladenis and Raymond Blanc – declined to do so.

We are the same age and we have been friends for more than ten years. I have never worked with Marco, and I am doing well in my own style, but without him I would not be where I am today. When I met that chap I was lost. I had taken a gamble to come to England – and then I saw that Marco was facing the same problems. Because I am French I saw what he was doing, against the mass of convention in this country. I needed to know how to do it, and Marco showed me. He is generous and kind. And he was ten years ahead of his time.

Marco analyses things. He quickly understands the essentials of a problem. Some people are leaders, others need to be led. He is Napoleon, I am Lafayette! I understood him from day one. Marco doesn't do it for ego, or for money, but for the sake of doing it. He understands tradition. At 22, he was already a star, though he seemed ten years older; yet he had to fight and to suffer disappointments. The English didn't know what he was doing: I knew because I am French. He is always news. He has extraordinary commitment and involvement with what he does.

He is a combination of so many elements. He is the Fernand Point of this country. You know, all the top chefs of France were trained by Point. Well, every top chef in England worked for Marco. With him, there is always more to come. He is a great creator. He could have done anything in life.

You know, I am fit, very fit I think. But Marco! One day we were walking in Hyde Park. A dog ran away from its owner. Impossible to catch it. But Marco was off. Half an hour later, he is back, with the dog in his arms.

The death of his mother left him with a need. He has to compensate. Once we drove past the Hyde Park Hotel and he said, "One day my name will be on that awning!" I would cut off my hand for that chap.

– Jean-Christophe Novelli

I knocked on Marco's door at Harvey's, aged 19, and asked for a job. It was there I was instilled with a love and understanding of food. I knew him better than anybody, but as an individual, not as a trainee. I warmed to his generosity. He had phenomenal energy, ideas, creativeness. Marco gets bored very easily – so he has to move on. He has incredible drive. He sets the highest standards, and he has the team to do it. He looks after his staff, and pays. Marco makes his chefs feel safe as houses: he is the best chef-manipulator!

– Gordon Ramsay

Marco is very intelligent, a very kind man – some of it perhaps for effect. I've never known if it's genuine. I always wanted to be his friend. If only he would let people be his friends! Marco followed in Nico's [Ladenis's] footsteps with bad behaviour to get attention – underneath, he's a very nice guy. A real man.

I was very interested in Alex, his first wife. And in Mati, when she was running the bar at The Canteen. So I lost out to Marco twice! He has mellowed a lot, since Mati, but he still doesn't like women journalists. He likes to shock instantly. He had Shane Prince [of the *Daily Telegraph*] in tears once. He likes his artwork though – nice collection.

To me, he's neglected by society. It's ridiculous! He has never even been given a catering award. He deserves more than he's been given for what he has done for our trade. An OBE at least. They're frightened. Imagine him with the Queen! *He* is the queen bee: the world comes to Marco, Marco doesn't go to the world.

I've never gone the Michelin route. Michelin puts you on the spot: like telling people to go and see a certain film – they mightn't like it! (Funny, there's never been a naughty chef in France.) We date from the same time, and I think he respects me as a survivor. Marco is the most talented chef Britain has ever produced.

If I needed help and went to him, he would give it to me. He has been cruel at times: some men have a death-wish, push people away. A very pleasant guy – if he would let people like him, he would be a better man.

– Anthony Worrall Thompson

I was cooking at Gravetye Manor and took my girlfriend up to Yorkshire to stay the night and dine at the Box Tree on February 14, 1980. After dinner, we went into the kitchen to chat to the chef. There were five or six people there, and one of them was Marco. He hung back, but you noticed him. Then I went to work for the Roux brothers at Gavvers, which had been the Gavroche, and there was another commis-chef there I thought I recognized. I started to say, "Haven't we met somewhere …" and Marco – that's who it was – said, "The Box Tree, Valentine's Day, 1980." Then he went through the menu we had had that night: every detail!

His foundation was the Box Tree: other places have been significant, but not as much as the Box Tree. Marco idolized Albert. Raymond Blanc was important. Raymond has two stars, Marco three. Raymond has a fantastic hotel, but Marco focused on the food. He was always totally focused on what he wanted, he always knew what he wanted to do, even at 19.

We've always kept in touch. I went to see him at Harvey's. He hasn't changed – he has the same personality he had at 19.

– John McManus

I wanted to work for Marco because of his name and reputation. I knew it would be hard work but would make me stronger mentally and in terms of my cooking skills. When I went to see him at The Restaurant in the Hyde Park, he wasn't there – he was having his picture taken in the lounge, so he sent for me and said, "You're a nice-looking lad." I don't know if he was used to public-school boys, but I got the job.

When you work for Marco Pierre White you learn about absolute precision. His food is very clean, very light. A lot of work goes into what you do, but what ends up on the plate looks quite simple, very visual. There were days when it was such hard work at The Restaurant that I wanted to leave – when I started, I was working from 7.30 in the morning to 1.00 the next morning.

After nearly three years, I'd had enough. I took time out for six months. Then I met Marco at a party – most unusual, he never socializes outside his restaurants – when he was merging with Granada, and he offered me the Café Royal Grill. It had acquired a star under the previous chef, and most unusually, because of the respect they had for Marco, Michelin gave me three weeks to prove we deserved to keep it. I had three inspections in three weeks, the last by the head inspector, Derek Bulmer [who had replaced Derek Brown] – and we kept the star. Lucky!

– Spencer Patrick

mayfair mafioso

By the spring of 1998, as the daffodils and stripy deck-chairs blossomed in Green Park, a striking figure could be added to the busy denizens – doormen, postmen, cabbies, sweepers, policemen, messengers, club men – of London's West End. In the area bounded to the east by Soho and to the west by Hyde Park, and whose heart is glamorous Mayfair, regular sightings could be made of a tall (6 foot 3 inch), well-built (17 stone) man of 36, urgently hailing a taxi, clambering into a chauffeur-driven Range Rover or striding purposefully (on size 11 feet). Here, among the wandering tourists and engrossed shoppers, was someone who was always going somewhere, urgently. Here, in this small, packed arena, there were always matters that needed his attention, and places that needed his presence.

The more perceptive observers of this unusual personage – curly dark hair not so much combed as fingered, brown eyes not missing much, skin that could use some fresh air – would be able to deduce his line of business from his trademark garb. Under a tweed jacket of

---

vignette

He's very clever at using other people's money. Businessmen follow him, but at the end of the day he seems to have left a lot of his partners behind. As a businessman, he looks after number one.

– **Dominic Walsh, journalist,** *Sunday Business*

---

the kind favoured by the older aristocracy (and like theirs, tailored in Savile Row), of whose shoots, at Petworth and Blenheim, he was now a member, he wore a form-hugging chef's double-breasted white jacket. Instantly recognized by many a passing customer and by all cabbies ("I had that Marco in the back of my cab …"), England's greatest chef, if his peers are to be believed, was on his daily rounds.

The route went from Piccadilly Circus, straddled by the orientalist Criterion and the romantic Café Royal Grill, deep into Soho for the arty Quo Vadis, back down Piccadilly to the gastronomic shrine of the Oak Room: Marco's patch, tended with loving care by Marco's boys. (And now also by at least one girl: Mati, the mother of his sons, looked after the front of house at the Criterion, conveniently for the return home to Knightsbridge in the small hours, after Marco had finished service at the Oak Room.)

On this particular spring day, however, the destination would be Curzon Street, where Marco and his partner Jimmy Lahoud had acquired not one but two restaurants. The highly acclaimed Les Saveurs had been the first of these, but with the purchase of a second property, a mere hundred yards or so down the street, the partners decided that it would be prudent not to be in competition with themselves. They therefore offered Les Saveurs, at what the French call a friend's price, to Rocco Forte, who installed Marco's admirer, the rising star Jean-Christophe Novelli, as chef. It was the remaining restaurant, the Mirabelle, that now became the main object of Marco's famously focused attention.

"I've been offered places in New York and in Paris," Marco says, "but the only place I'd leave England for would be Maxim's – Maxim's the way it used to be. That was my dream. But the Mirabelle was the Maxim's of London, wasn't it? Well, now I own it!" The young commis-chef, in his earlier skinny, wild-boy persona, used to walk, between services, all the way from Le Gavroche in Chelsea to Curzon Street, just to gaze at the façade of the once-great restaurant. On one occasion he had had the temerity to go in and ask for the menu. Mayfair had always meant glamour and romance – at one end of

Curzon Street it was Spring in Park Lane and at the other A Nightingale Sang in Berkeley Square – and nothing in it was more glamorous than the Mirabelle, once London's only world-class restaurant. For Marco Pierre White, it had been love at first sight, "my little love affair". To put it another way, if the Oak Room was the beloved wife, the one you came home to, the Mirabelle would be the stunning mistress, the blonde on the side.

Inopportunely, the Mirabelle had opened in 1940, a time of blitz, hardship, shortages, ration books – but within a decade it was London's unashamedly élitist dinner destination. Table One, legend has it, was reserved for the wealthiest client of the night and Table Two was kept until 9pm, in case royalty showed, as it often did. By 1961, Egon Ronay (in his first-ever restaurant guide) had classed it with the Caprice, Coq d'Or, L'Ecu de France, Prunier's and the Savoy Grill Room as one of London's best restaurants:

> It has the smartest and richest clientele: it has to be both: smart, to
> fit into this gleaming décor accompanied by heavy silver, crystal,
> and all the miscellaneous catering trinkets of luxury; rich, for this is
> the most expensive restaurant in town. A double-edged asset this,
> and if you are only in the mink class and not the sable set, the place
> may give you a mink-feriority complex. The staff is of such skill and
> so smart that you suspect their motor cars are longer than yours.
> The cooking is very good. The wine list gives unqualified pleasure
> to all and overdrafts to some.

The glamour-quotient of the clientele was hard to top: Noel Coward, the Duke of Bedford, Sir Bernard and Lady Docker (gold Daimler no doubt parked outside), "Mr Five Per Cent", Nubar Gulbenkian (who preferred his private taxi to bring him the few hundred yards from his home in the Ritz), Maria Callas and Aristotle Onassis (who first met Jackie Kennedy there), Maurice Chevalier, Jean Cocteau, Cecil Beaton. You would meet the same crowd in First Class on the *Queen Mary* or the *Normandie*.

The Mirabelle's fate was more like that of an old and leaky tub: a slow, agonized sinking. Inevitably, that which depends on fashion goes out of fashion. The Mirabelle became mere premises, a site, a shell, passed from hand to hand. One owner brought in a chef to see what a bit of English *nouvelle cuisine* (alas, another fashion) could do. Another tried to get a casino licence for the place. The restaurant was finally bought by a group of Japanese businessmen, OTA Resources, who installed a teppanyaki bar *and* a French restaurant. This schizophrenic attempt to have their cake and eat it was, predictably, doomed, and the old place was back again on the market.

Potential buyers were known to be on the prowl, among them the shrewd and highly successful owners of the Ivy and the Caprice, Jeremy King and Chris Corbin. Their presence in the field may have been the reason for Marco's later – and typically provocative – claim that "I bought it not because I wanted it, but because I didn't want anyone else to have it". Matthew Fort of the *Guardian* was surely nearer the mark when he pointed out that the classical virtues of Marco Pierre White's cuisine translated neatly into the style of the restaurants with which he is associated:

> With the exception of MPW [now Big Chef] in Canary Wharf, the restaurants themselves are historic sites. Once, they were temples to traditional virtues, but, sadly, in recent years they had fallen into desuetude as a result of fading energies and changing fashions. If nothing else, Mr White should be congratulated on reviving the fortunes of, and making accessible, some of the most remarkable dining rooms in London, the luxury of which would be impossible to build from scratch these days.

More graphically, Jonathan Meades of *The Times* declared:

> It's almost inevitable that the man to exhume it [the Mirabelle] should be Marco Pierre White. Whilst Conran builds his own nests

– he is, after all, a designer – White circles like a vulture with cuckooish tendencies and preys on grandiose decrepitude. The Criterion, the Oak Room and the Café Royal Grill are sites of ancient splendour. And the same goes for the Mirabelle …

Whatever the motivations behind it, the acquisition of the Mirabelle was an undoubted financial coup. Marco's publicly stated claim is that he paid £1.4 million for the restaurant and wine cellar (lavishly replenished by the Japanese owners), as against the rival offer of £1.6 million, *without* the cellar, from Messrs King and Corbin. Another explanation for his triumph, again from Marco, is that the Japanese preferred his offer because, in an inspired moment during negotiations, he spontaneously offered to guarantee their manager, Takanori Ishii, a job for life. (There may well have been a self-serving motive: this industrious gentleman, always respectfully addressed by Marco as "Mr Ishii", has become his indispensable right-hand man.)

Perhaps the niftiest element in the deal was that Marco became the personal owner of the lease of the premises – with a fixed rent of a derisory £20 a week – and then rented it to his (and Jimmy Lahoud's) company, MPW-Criterion Ltd. This "hidden asset" alone is said to be worth £4 million.

An even better-concealed asset, according to Marco's Mayfair neighbour, David Coffer, was the fabled wine cellar. "Worth half as much as he paid for the restaurant," Coffer says, speaking in the boardroom of his company offices in Albemarle Street (handily placed for lunchtime excursions to any of Marco's establishments). "Go on – ask him about that. He *pinched* that wine cellar."

Coffer is probably the country's leading restaurant broker, and when the Mirabelle came on the market, Marco asked him to look into the possibilities for him. "I knew Jimmy Lahoud from way back and he introduced us, at the Criterion. I was enchanted by Marco's charisma. An extraordinary man. And a highly intelligent businessman. His ability to negotiate is astonishing – and I've seen them all. I was impressed by his ability to bid the right price. Marco knows what it's about. I'm proud to be his mate, even if it is a bit like walking in a lion's den." Marco was, according to the robust but cultivated Coffer, "born with class". The restaurants are a product of that: "Restaurants are many things – eating places, warehouses, properties – but their lifeblood is *theatre*. Go into any of Marco's places: it's pure theatre. I've never seen anything like it, and I've been in this business for 33 years."

What kind of a show would Marco put on at the Mirabelle? In the spring of 1998, gutted to its bare bones, the place looked like what it was: a long basement below a characterless block of service flats. At its extremity it had, however, an open terrace and, since the main room was situated in the well of the building, it had sky above it. David Collins had been the house architect since the days of Harvey's and was called in again here, but observers had little doubt about whose baby this was going to be.

The Marx Brothers would have admired the bedlam, and indeed there was a camera crew on hand to record it, if they could only get their lenses on the leading man. Marco's new mantra may have been "affordable glamour", but this was going to be glamour at whatever the cost: those in the know quoted a total of £4 million. Here, for example, in bricky London W1, there would be not merely a garden, but a Provençal one.

The floor would be oak parquet, but as soon as it was laid it was clear to the master builder Marco that it wasn't *right*. Fortunately, he had discovered another one, a 17th-century French job called *parquet de Versailles,* so the first one was torn up and replaced with the classy import. The banquettes turned out to be too deep, and so were truncated. Then their leather covering was found to be the wrong shade of brown and the quality not high enough, so the Rolls-Royce upholsterers, Connolly, were called in and the whole thing done again. One of the private rooms would be decorated in gold leaf for a Chinese effect, and the other would have a leather floor, for its opulence and rich smell. "Let there be light," Marco had murmured, so there would be cheerful skylights, and also a long bar, and perhaps a piano, and certainly chandeliers. There would surely be art from Marco's growing collection.

Then there were the knick-knacks, those little touches that punch above their weight in conferring personality. Marco, on a visit to L'Escargot, owned by Jimmy Lahoud, found himself seated next to a free-standing silver wine-bucket which, his observant eye noticed, was engraved with the legendary name of his new property. Acquiring the piece, he had it copied in quantity by his old school chum, Marcus Steel, who now had a studio in Birmingham. Marco's flower-lady, Annabel Grey, visiting a friend, spotted one of the original Mirabelle ashtrays. Finding it pretty, Marco had it copied too. (When, following the opening, the ashtrays failed to disappear from tables at a satisfactory rate, Marco had them inscribed on the back "Property of Marco Pierre White": that did the trick.)

The glamour would be assured, but there remained the problem of making it affordable – without sacrificing the quality associated with the now famous new owner's name. Marco brought in two of his "boys" as head chefs: Lee Bunting, who had been with him for 12 years, and Charlie Rushton, an eight-year veteran. With them, testing and tasting, he worked on a menu that would combine, at reasonable prices, tried and trusted classics from the Marco Pierre White repertoire with others, sometimes cheerfully filched from elsewhere – and given the Marco spin. (Writing about a visit to the Savoy Grill, the *Spectator*'s critic, David Fingleton, felt obliged to report of one of its celebrated creations that "alas, the definitive Omelette Arnold Bennett is now at the Mirabelle".)

Marco's *Tatler* editor friend Jane Procter having decided to celebrate the opening, guests from the magazine's constantly amended and refined list of movers and cocktail shakers gathered in the refurbished premises one evening in early May 1998. Outside, the name "Mirabelle" in glowing thirties-style blue-neon script announced the return of glamour to this corner of Mayfair. Rocco Forte strolled down from a private dinner party at Les Saveurs and was a little surprised to find his chef, Jean-Christophe Novelli, there before him, leaning on the bar with his latest girlfriend. But he was not at all surprised not to find his friend Marco there. Marco, who earlier that day had been on his knees fixing a recalcitrant section of the antique parquet, had decided to dine quietly elsewhere with Mati and a few friends, arriving nearer midnight than the appointed hour of six o'clock. A good time, reportedly, was had by all, but the true test would come on the morrow. Would the targeted punters come? And what would the critics have to say?

First signs were far from good. True to British press tradition, the *Express*, perhaps mistaking the premises for the equally faceless former MI5 headquarters opposite, sent along their political correspondent, Siòn Simon, who had this stern warning for his readers: "Unless you like being patronized, insulted and consistently messed about, don't go to the Mirabelle," an establishment where, he reported, "the staff were completely hopeless". Although he grudgingly conceded that the place was "a nice enough hangout, in a smart part of town, to keep the middle-aged perma-tans going back for more lobster and scallops", it was hard to square this with the sober conclusion of that respected pro Fay Maschler of the *Evening Standard*: "London has been given back one of the glories of its restaurant history."

At the 1999 Carlton London Restaurant Awards, the Mirabelle was chosen as the Best New Restaurant of the Year. (True to form, Marco failed to appear to collect the bauble, sending along in his place the young Charlie Rushton. Rushton's nicely delivered acceptance speech consisted of one, deeply appreciated sentence: "Well, here we are again, waiting for Marco.")

Maschler's conclusion, quoted above, was almost trumped by her opening sentences: "If you have any doubts that Marco Pierre White is a phenomenon, his relaunched Mirabelle will dispel them. A lot of nonsense is talked by New Age people about individuals who possess an old soul but, in restoring and revivifying what was one of the great gastronomic addresses of London, Marco has proved that at some point, for a while anyway, he must have been Napoleon, Carême and Fred Astaire."

Even after the opening, it seemed, these three distinguished chaps, in their present singular form, were still attending to the details (where, we are told, God is to be found): "When I went to the Mirabelle, indecently early in its new life," reported Maschler, "he [Marco] was on his hands and knees rubbing polish into the herringbone oak parquet floors, as were the troops, his members of staff. When the food arrived it was as steadily brilliant, as delicate in its revelations, as only culinary knowledge won through years of hard graft can produce."

It is worth staying with Fay Maschler's observations, for they deal perceptively with each of Marco's sometimes stated, sometimes cautiously concealed aims for this, his first establishment created – name apart – truly from scratch. "The various rooms, which have been woken from a long, dull sleep into a kind of beauty, provide a definition of glamour. Glamour depends utterly on someone's passion. It is the addiction to the job that provides the faultless footwork which dazzles." Pointing out that Marco, having proved that he knew how to cook, wanted to show that he knew how to eat, Maschler noted that "few chefs – in fact it is hard to think of another – who perform alchemy in the kitchen also think about the way daylight will gleam on silvered wallpaper or understand how the scent of a leather floor or the slide show provided by mirrored doors can contribute to the enjoyment of being in a room". As for the affordability of the undoubted glamour: "Marco wanted it to be accessible. To this end, the long menu of what are now his own classics has first courses priced from £6.50 for, say, truffled parsley soup with poached egg (brilliant, by the way), or Omelette Arnold Bennett, and main courses from £11.50 for smoked haddock with Jersey Royals and beurre blanc."

Maschler's colleague Nick Foulkes, writing in the *Evening Standard*'s weekly magazine, *ES,* also wondered at "Marco Pierre White's almost magical capacity to revive even the most dead and buried of restaurants and re-invent them as high-fashion dining destinations". The White magic seemed to work al fresco too, or anyway "makes a noble attempt to replicate the ambience of Provence with tiers of lavender, rosemary and olives. There are even a few vines in the corner ..."

Entering what had been "merely a protracted dungeon", the *Times* man, Jonathan Meades, was impressed by *trompe l'oeil* bookshelves by Pierre Le Tain, and the glamour achieved by "just a few judicious touches", like "a mirrored hanging globe from Regine's, 1940s mirrored screens, a curiously textured wallpaper which achieves its effects through light and shadow, vast displays of flowers, abundant applications of silver leaf ..." Adding that "the food is fabulous", he marked the place, as he had The Restaurant at the Hyde Park (before maxing it out on a second visit), at 9 out of 10.

Gallantly recovering from the shock of first impressions – "you come into a small lobby that's like the entrance to a plastics factory in the Midlands that's on the skids" – Michael Winner informed his *Sunday Times* readers that "Marco Pierre White's newly opened Mirabelle restaurant in London's Mayfair is staggeringly good and great value ... and the à la carte meal I had in the garden was one of the best ever".

David Fingleton of the *Spectator* basked under "the sloping, frosted-glass skylights" and in "the gorgeous inner-city walled garden", declaring it to be "truly a dream of a place". *Square Meal* found "power and drama in equal measure, a fine mix of tempered opulence and beauty", and decided that the cooking was "no less dramatic".

Matthew Fort of the *Guardian* nostalgically recalled that his parents once lived in a service flat above the old Mirabelle which, through "a curious quirk of the lease" was obliged to send food up on demand. "My mother says that she has never lived so well in her life as during those days of rationing." Today her son – who also contrives to live pretty well – reports that "the menu is a clever mix of retro simple, retro classic and MPW retro" and that "the place has grace and space and light. It glows with understated, even joky, good taste, and, as long as you keep away from the mad end of the monster wine list [he may have had in mind the Château d'Yquem at £30,000] the bill should be surprisingly reasonable."

The man had done it again. Rarely can the opening of a new restaurant, anywhere, have evinced such universal approval. "The Mirabelle is a great achievement of which Marco is rightly proud," said Michael Winner, adding that "Marco Pierre White is highly talented and amusing. He's also nutty, machiavellian, mercurial, utterly childish, irrational and dangerous. All qualities I greatly admire."

Reciprocating these fine, if cagily qualified, sentiments, Marco invited Winner to cut the ribbon at the launch of his new venture, the Titanic. The restaurant was cheekily so called (by who else but the intrepid, fate-tempting Marco?) because it would be sited above the Atlantic, a highly fashionable bar and grill at the back of Granada's deeply unfashionable Regent Palace Hotel, which was, however, nicely placed within the frontiers of the rapidly expanding MPW empire. This, a 600-seater, bar-disco-club-restaurant, would be the severest test yet of Marco's claim that "I can sell quality to volume". The rakish Titanic would be moored a rope's throw from the flagship, the stout Oak Room, but its concept of affordable food and fun would be light years away from that of the gastronomic shrine. The feisty Irishman Oliver Peyton, himself something of a street fighter (and the husband, as it happened, of Rocco Forte's niece), further maintained it would be in direct competition with the below-stairs Atlantic, which he owned. Would the Titanic be swallowed by the Atlantic? Would it hit the iceberg of the recession many were predicting? While the press posed these questions – "Atlantic could sink Titanic in London bar-room squall" – Marco, as was his habit, remained buoyant, and busy.

•••

"My philosophy is that a person should always expand in a recession because there's more opportunity and everything is cheaper. Expanding in a boom is expensive and is therefore against my philosophy." This was Marco Pierre White's response to a journalist (Pete Clark of the *Evening Standard*, whose seriousness can be measured by the fact that he took mints along to the interview purely so that he could offer one with the question, "Polo, Marco?") who had questioned the wisdom of launching a vast new vessel on economic waters which, although apparently calm, might reveal, just over the horizon, the threatening iceberg of recession. What do people do in a recession? Marco asked, and had the answer: "They cancel the extension on the house, they cancel the redecoration, they cancel the new car – but they still want to go out and feed!"

Although the Titanic would be, in Marco's provocatively understated description, "a pub with a restaurant attached", the huge room off Brewer Street would, in fact, provide drinking space for 350 and eating space for 220. Although it pleased him to announce, "I am now a publican," he knew that the feeding of the multitude, even after his experience of cooking for large numbers at The Canteen, would be a serious challenge. His aim was to serve three courses for "around 20 quid": proper food with no unnecessary frills, which, after all, was what he had claimed to be serving at whatever level of establishment. "I am a classicist. I say that if you serve the best fish and chips in the world you deserve an award. To produce the best bacon in the world is gastronomy."

It was not, however, Marco the new publican who was now called reluctantly into action, but an older model, Marco the well-known litigant, though this time more sued against than suing. Already locked in battle with no less an adversary than the *New York Times*, whose restaurant reviewer had ill-advisedly made reference to Marco's former "well-publicized bout with drugs and alcohol" when he is notorious in celebrity-land for eschewing such popular palliatives, he now heard the whistle of a shot across the bows of the Titanic. As the *Sunday Times* reported the matter: "Oliver Peyton, owner of the Atlantic Bar and Grill, once one of London's trendiest places to be seen, has served a High Court writ on Marco Pierre White, the celebrity chef noted for his less than ice-cool temper." Peyton, who, as the owner of three restaurants, Coast, Mash, and Mash and Air, was something of a rival empire-builder, claimed that an exclusion clause prevented his landlord – none other than the Granada group with whom Marco was so fondly linked – from letting the former ballroom above his premises to a competitive restaurant. (Spice was added to the altercation when it emerged that the spokespeople for the adversaries were ex-husband and wife Alan Crompton-Batt for Marco and Elizabeth Crompton-Batt for Peyton.)

"We are in the ballroom; the Atlantic is in the morgue," said Alan Crompton-Batt, helpfully. Peyton's PR made it clear that "our dispute is not with Marco Pierre White but with our landlords". Peyton declared, "I don't have a problem with Marco, he's one of the greatest cooks in Britain, but he has sold his soul to Little Chef." Marco responded magnanimously: "Oliver is a very clever boy. What he's doing is applying his nightclub mentality to running a restaurant. He's got the place full of city boys at 6pm, then full of the idle rich until 3am. I think the Atlantic is a brilliant name too. It sounds trendy, massive and well-established, all at the same time." The *Sunday Times* reporter summed up by quoting Marco's PR man again: "The Atlantic is saying that there cannot be a similar operation in the building and Marco is saying b******s." Marco's view, if somewhat inelegantly expressed, prevailed.

The refurbishment went on too, and the tall, powerful, tweeded, corded, white-breasted addition to the Mayfair fauna could now be spotted making his majestic way between the cigar-scented glamour of the Mirabelle, where he now held daily court, the hallowed halls of the Oak Room, where he cooked the three-star dinner, and the dusty, chaotic building site of the Titanic, where he generously put the long-suffering David Collins right on matters of architecture and décor. (On his rounds, friends report, he has been known to stop the taxi, hop out and press a large note into the hand of a down-and-out in a doorway: not, he claims, for show or even from compassion, but as a sort of investment – he feels he has thus bought the right to accept hand-outs should he ever find himself similarly destitute.)

The ballroom of the Regent Palace had once been a stately, gracious place, the perfect setting for men in tails and women in long gowns. Its sky-blue ceiling had been modelled on that of the *Queen Mary*'s First Class dining room and its walls were richly panelled. Sadly, all this beauty and craftsmanship had been buried in decades of plastification as the hotel succumbed to the pressures of mass tourism and the great room became that tawdry symbol of would-be authenticity, a "carvery".

Marco's target market, of course, was hardly the toff and his lady from older times. On the contrary, as one journalist put it: "Now that he has got the well-heeled and the high-heeled, he wants the hip as well." But "affordable glamour" was the rallying cry of the moment, and the glamour would be supplied by the surroundings. Then there was Marco's conviction that this could be achieved without lowering the high standards he had hitherto, and indisputably, set. "Supplying quality to volume" was the challenge here, and that applied to the menu too. There might be the waggishly titled "Steak Hâché à la McDonald's" and another American import, Caesar salad, but there would also be smoked salmon with blinis and roast pheasant with bread sauce. The *brigade* of Marco's boys was headed by Lee Bunting, indoctrinated since Harvey's days, and now the leader of the designated task force that opened up new establishments as to the manner trained, and then moved on.

A happy discovery was that the owners of the unhappy *SS Titanic* had been the White Star Line, and the multi-starred Mr White seized on the coincidence to make a small white star the motif of the establishment. Ever the snapper-up of unconsidered trifles, Marco also acquired the year of the disaster, 1912, as the last four digits of the restaurant's telephone number.

Once again, it was the *Tatler* that pushed the boat out, making the second launch of the Titanic the pretext for its 1998 Christmas party. (The invitations announced the theme: "Overdressed and Overboard".) One paper excitedly reported that "all the *Tatler* girls wore long dresses with jewels, while the cigarette girls were squeezed into naughty turn-of-the-century style corset dresses". The *Evening Standard* awarded 5 out of 5 for the "glam quotient" which "could hardly have been hipper. With a Rolling Stone, a Genesis, a Pink Floyd and Bob Geldof in one corner, the All Saints in the other, the Marquess of Blandford running the bar, the Marquess of Milford Haven sipping champagne next to Goldie", a good time was apparently had by all. "Planet Hollywood with waves," was one guest's description. There were even reported sightings of Marco Pierre White himself, and one unfortunate journalist, who had incurred the owner's displeasure by asking intrusive questions, confirmed his presence: "'You have been invited here as my guest and you are very rude to abuse that position,' he [Marco] declared. 'You're going to have to leave,' he said grimly, moving his hand on to my shoulder and propelling me through the crowd with his considerable bulk."

The more serious journalists waited for calmer seas. The novelist and *Evening Standard* columnist Sebastian Faulks mused, "Londoners can always sense the approach of Christmas. The weather becomes warm and wet, children come home from school with interesting new viruses, Marco Pierre White opens a new restaurant from which he evicts a journalist." Noting that the menu had borrowed the last words of the *Titanic*'s captain – "Be British" – Faulks observed that the food was more British than the staff or customers, although he couldn't put a nationality to the "Steak Hâché à la McDonald's". However, "the burger was big, meaty and rare, the chips plump and starchy. It cost £9.50, which is probably six times what you'd pay for a McDonald's, but it was six times as big and 20 times as nice." His authentically hip companion, "a world expert in Caesar salads", gave the Titanic's version 9 out of 10 and "the roast pheasant a similar thumbs-up. It may be the first time that bread sauce has been described as wicked." All in all, it was – puns being irresistible in this context – "the coolest dive in town".

Faulks's foxier colleague, Nick Foulkes, in a serious restaurant review, was no more immune: "After all, Marco Pierre White's splashiest (oops) launch (sorry) happens to be named after one of the great maritime – and cinematic – disasters of the century. The Titanic, however, shows little sign of being a disaster. When I have swung by on a couple of recent evenings, the place has been heaving, which is as it should be, because Titanic is basically a huge bar and nightclub thinly disguised as a restaurant." Conceding that "there is food, of course", Foulkes warned that "fat cats and gastro bores hoping to get the type of Michelin-influenced restaurant pageantry and highfalutin, high-cost cuisine that prevails at Marco Pierre White's Oak Room or the delightful subterranean Mirabelle will be disappointed. No, Titanic is the sort of place where you get Bang Bang Chicken for £6.50 ... and the emphasis on late-night hedonism is stressed by the inclusion of a breakfast menu which is served from 11.30pm to 2.30am."

"Titanic is a generation thing," Foulkes concludes. "If you are over 25 and/or allergic to loud music, visit it at lunchtime. But try it after dark if you want the full-on rock 'n' roll experience of dimmed lighting, sparkling mirror balls, ferocious din, and the kind of atmosphere that used to prevail at such sprawling pleasure palaces as Studio 54 in its heyday."

Having noted at the Carlton London Restaurant Awards dinner that "this *überchef* was so busy greeting diners [at the Titanic] that he failed to turn up to receive his own award for Best New Restaurant for Mirabelle", Alice Thompson of the *Spectator* concluded that "either he had stayed to man a sinking ship, or the party on board was too good". Having, with difficulty, booked a table at the Titanic, she found that the décor looked "suitably theme-ish ... the lamps were brassy, the leatherette seats sticky, and the music sounded as if we were standing next to the steam-engine room of an extremely large vessel. A blue sea seemed to lap above us in an alarming way ... [and] the vast room was already heaving with nubile teenagers in spaghetti straps and ankle chains."

As for the food, "the menu couldn't have been the one on offer in first, second or third class on the *Titanic*. It was a hotchpotch. There was a salad of crispy duck for Chinese fanatics, blinis with smoked salmon for Russian passengers, and linguini of clams for the Italians." Although "the service was fantastic", sadly (the "generation thing", no doubt), "the whole experience was more of an ordeal than a treat". To make up, Ms Thompson vowed to take her guests to the Mirabelle: "Now that is an elegant restaurant. The seats are deep, the food is sublime, and it doesn't have a silly name."

Strictures on the décor were not confined to the critics: Marco wasn't happy either. The whole entrance needed changing. The colour of the walls wasn't right. He had an idea for new drinks tables, using the white star. There ought to be mobiles. Six months after the launch, the shipwrights were back and Captain Marco was on day-watch on the bridge. He had, of course, other things on his mind as well.

Court circular

Although Marco at 36 could reasonably claim to live "a simple life" – which the journalist Lynn Barber was pleased to interpret in her usual barbed way as "a simple flat in Knightsbridge, a simple country house on a famous fishing lake in Hampshire, a simple Range Rover ..." – the smooth running of his activities outside the kitchen depended on a small, loyal, if long-suffering entourage. Here, a few of them recount their experiences:

> I first met him at a party in Quo Vadis, given by Jane Procter. In fact, it was in his honour, given to launch a book of his, I think. Marco arrived late, slipped in right at the end, and just sat there, looking terribly shy, not comfortable at all. Then, after he had read an article about me in one of the Sunday papers, I got a call: "Come to the Oak Room!" There, in his own domain, he was completely different. He was Louis the 14th, or Picasso, holding court, completely at ease, charming, hugely generous.
>
> He's a star, very creative, with enormous energy put into whatever he does. The *look* of his restaurants, the colours – he has a

very good eye. Not many restaurateurs have a talent for cooking *and* for decoration. Anyway, cooking is an art form: Marco doesn't regard it as such, but it is. He doesn't go for the cheap option. There's a feel of quality in the Mirabelle – the most elegant restaurant in London, and, like Marco, very romantic.

I was sitting there one day with a group at one of the large tables and Marco cut into somebody's conversation to ask me, "Have you seen my hippo?" This was one of the Bugatti sculptures he had been collecting. I said, "No, where is it?" and it turned out it was in the Oak Room. Marco got on the phone and said, "Take a taxi!" and 20 minutes later some poor man staggered in with this huge beast. Marco told him to put it on the end of a nearby table and told him to keep the taxi. It just sat there for half an hour while the conversation went on and then Marco said, "Take it away." When he got the *Tatler Restaurant Guide*'s award for Best Newcomer for the Mirabelle, he knew I'd been invited and said one day, "I've told them you will be collecting it." *

He knows the value of flamboyant gestures, that they will boost his reputation. He makes you feel you are the most important person in the world – but he is not calculating. He is very decisive, but likes to keep other people waiting. I wanted to paint his picture and call it *Portrait of a Madman*. I would paint it for me, not for him – I wouldn't want to jeopardize our friendship with anything commercial. He was all for it, but how to get hold of him to sit? I have to plan things months ahead, but Marco will only plan days ahead. Getting Marco to do anything outside his own territory is like trying to give a cat a bath!
– **Jonny Yeo, painter, artistic adviser**

Impossible to read his mind. Once I went up to Leeds to look at the Queen's Hotel, where he will be opening a restaurant. When I went outside to photograph the façade I noticed that there was a

---

* Marco's framed award hangs on the wall of Yeo's studio.

nightclub right next door to where the restaurant entrance would be and I thought, "Oh, my God" and went in to telephone Marco straight away. He said, "Wonderful!"

– Takanori Ishii, special personal assistant

Things weren't moving fast enough with the work on the Mirabelle and I was introduced to Jimmy and Marco and it gelled. I respect Marco for what he has achieved, but we have our differences. What he can't understand is that he knows exactly what he wants, as in his cooking, but here he is up against building materials and their limitations. He has an excellent eye, though it's untrained. His appreciation of things is first class, but he gets frustrated and strides off. After a while he comes back and you can explain things. Then when you explain something, he starts to imagine it and when he sees the final result he is disappointed.

I try to control the budget, but this [the Mirabelle] is *Marco's* place. Here we went for everything. When it isn't quite right, he changes it, which means spending more money, but he knows he'll get it back in the long run. I can't think of another restaurateur that would put in a leather floor. It's very sexy, different. Marco's attitude is, if it doesn't look right, we'll pull it up! I can't think what's going to happen at the Titanic in the last two weeks when he sees it's not what he had imagined.* But for the Titanic, when we show Marco the banquette, for instance, I want the table in front of it, and the places set, just as they would be. In a sense, it's me understanding what Marco has *seen* in his mind's eye.

Marco made the effort of meeting us, of involving us, of inviting us to the Oak Room, showing us the menu [for the Mirabelle], took time to establish the relationship. I can't think of many people who would take that trouble.

– John Rowland, project manager

---

* Three months after the opening, Rowland and his team were back at the Titanic, changing things.

Marco and I have a lot in common: well, we're both working-class boys.* I worked for a lot of the top Savile Row firms before I decided to set up on my own. A customer of mine, Richard Edwards, who was also a customer and old friend of Marco's, wanted to give him a present, so he asked me to go round to the Hyde Park Hotel, ask for Marco, measure him up for a tweed jacket and send the bill to Richard.

Marco liked the jacket and that was the beginning. Well, Marco had been working hard all this time building up his business and hadn't had the opportunity before to have something for himself so he probably said, "I'm going to treat myself!" That's the sort of person he is. He was like a boy in a sweet shop where everything is free. In two and a half years I must have made him 20 jackets, 18 trousers, seven overcoats, plus suits. That's a colossal order. People just don't order on that scale. A lot of people with a biggish order try to knock you down [on price]. Not Marco.

He hasn't changed size since I started making for him. Once we had the most horrendous row. I knew I hadn't done anything wrong, and he soon came round. I know the pressures he's under, so I don't take these things too seriously. Marco is just an all-round nice guy. He seems to know when I'm going through a bad patch and sends in an order to help me out. He has helped me when I've had liquidity worries. No matter how busy he is, if you go to him and say, "Marco, I've got a problem," he'll drop everything and listen. Often that's all you need – someone to listen.

– Dougie Davis, tailor

Marco phoned me up one day and talked for about an hour and a half! I think one of his chefs had bought venison from the estate and that's how he knew about me. We have a lot of things in common. We both lost our mothers at the age of six. Another thing we have in common is that Marco always wanted to be a gamekeeper!

---

* Dougie Davis drives a Rolls-Royce.

The first thing I noticed about Marco was his knowledge of nature. He really *knew* about the birds. He wants to give his boys an appreciation of wildlife. He works for his family, just as I do – he's always going on about Mati or the boys. Mati is a lovely lady: they're both lovely people.

Marco pays great attention to detail. Before he ever went on a shoot, he insisted on going on the range to become fully competent with the rifle – not just the handling but the etiquette. Before he ever started, he must have come down [to Petworth] at least six times. He always wants to improve. He insists on having a gamekeeper beside him to correct and criticize. He has the best equipment. He likes very fine things and he can afford it.

I don't think he fits into any category. I would count Marco among my friends, though we're miles apart in wealth. He chooses to mix with all sorts, but he never forgets his roots, never forgets his friends: he fishes on the lake at Petworth with Tim Steel, his classmate in primary school.

I've never met anybody more generous – to everybody. I call it the Marco Pierre White redistribution of wealth system! The best meal I ever had in my life was in the Oak Room: Marco asked me and my wife for her birthday – a fantastic thing to do. He's very observant. The first time my wife met Marco – whom she adores – she said to me, "That man misses nothing."

– David Whitby, head gamekeeper, Petworth

I met Marco socially. I lived near Petworth and the first time I saw him he was landing four enormous fish from the lake! I like to shoot – fishing is too isolated, but for Marco it relieves him of the frustrations of work. Then, by chance, when I moved up to London, we were neighbours. I'm a tenant of the Duke of Westminster and I drive for the estate, and I drive for Marco [who doesn't drive] when he needs me.

When there are just two of you in a vehicle for long drives, you get to know somebody, on both sides of the fence, business and social. Marco doesn't like being spoken to when he is in a rage. If you like someone, you go along with it. It's like being married – if your wife gets in a mood … Marco eventually calms down. When he is with close friends, they can criticize him, advise him. But when he's with a social group, you know he's Prime Minister – he likes to be in control.

Marco's on a learning curve. He didn't have an education and he's getting one now. But he stays Marco – he still clowns around. He's in transition between super-chef and businessman-millionaire. Most people he knows are in his own empire – he ignores people outside it. Recently I spent three weeks with him at his home in Hampshire, with his daughter Lettie. That was the real Marco, going to fish-and-chip shops, always polite to people, giving money to people in the street – too much money, in my opinion. Once we were on a bus, and there was an old man scratching around in his purse for pennies to pay the fare, and as we got off, Marco stuffed a £50 note in his pocket. His generosity doesn't come from his being rich – he is *naturally* generous.

I've seen a real change in him. Before, he was behind closed doors all the time. Now he is more central to things, he is coming out, he is less isolated. He is forming his own club. He has an insatiable need to manage, but although he is surrounded by a court, he remains alone with his thoughts. He has two tiers of friends, business and private. He has a tremendous memory, too, and a very sharp intellect. And observation! A couple of days ago, we were leaving the Mirabelle and he was going to the nearby Range Rover and I was heading off to the distant Land Rover. "Your number plate's gone," Marco said. It was 100 yards away!

When I climb into that vehicle with him and we drive off, he is still the old Marco – if he loses that, he's lost everything he's gained. He's a nice bloke – as long as he remains so, I'm his friend.

– Bernard Lawson, driver

first days of empire

From *The Times*, 28th July 1998:

Fast foodie catches thief on night run

BY MARK HENDERSON

A LONG night took an unexpected course for the chef Marco Pierre White when he arrived from work during a burglary at his flat. As the burglar fled from the back door, Mr White decided to make use of his former skills as a cross-country runner and gave chase.

For a mile from Knightsbridge to Chelsea, the startled burglar, Glen Banks, 29 and slim-built, could not shake off the three-star Michelin chef, aged 35 and weighing 15 stone. Banks dropped his haul in the street, but still the chef kept gaining ground and alerted officers from a passing police car to join in the chase.

Banks was detained a short distance away, sweating profusely and heavily out of breath, a court was told yesterday as Mr White was praised for his courage. Unknown to him, Banks was a heroin user with a record including firearms offences.

He had stolen property worth £20,000 after he noticed an open window at Mr White's flat in Pavilion Road last Saturday morning. His haul included clothing, jewellery, two sets of car keys, three cameras, and handbags and sunglasses belonging to Mr White's girlfriend, Mati Conejero. At 3.55am, the couple arrived at the flat to find the lights on. Peter Zinner, for the prosecution, told Horseferry Road Magistrates' Court, "They were alarmed, and Miss Conejero unlocked the door as loudly as possible to alert the intruder and allow him to escape. That had the desired effect.

"Mr White realized that the premises had been burgled and, very bravely you may think, he went out into the street to confront the defendant. A hot pursuit continued and, on the way, Mr Banks dropped the bag in the street as he was aware that Mr White was making good ground."

After the arrest, the bag of stolen items was recovered and Banks, from Fulham, was found to have some items still on him. He pleaded guilty to burglary charges and was sent for sentence to Southwark Crown Court. He was denied bail.

Mr White, a former Yorkshire schoolboy running champion, runs prestigious restaurants such as the Oak Room and the Criterion. Banks has served sentences for burglary, robbery and shotgun offences. His lawyer, Robert Roscoe, agreed that "were it not for the diligence of Mr White in pursuing him, he might have got away without having any contact with the persons concerned".

From the *Evening Standard,* 4th September 1998:

Burglar gets five years despite chef Marco's mercy plea

BY PAUL CHESTON, COURTS CORRESPONDENT

CELEBRITY chef Marco Pierre White today appealed for mercy for the burglar he chased for a mile through west London to save £20,000 worth of his valuables. The appeal, however, was rejected at Southwark Crown Court when armed robber Glen Banks, of Fulham Road, was sentenced to five years for the raid on Mr White's Knightsbridge home ...

"We ran flat out for about a mile. I didn't think of the dangers, or that he might be armed. As I gained on him, sprinting like hell, I knew I wanted to catch him, to win, like it was a race. When I caught up with him, he just gave up quietly. He seemed sad and pathetic. I felt sorry for him. He seemed a bit undernourished." The 36-year-old Marco Pierre White's recollection of his widely reported chase after the unwisely intrusive burglar usefully encapsulates many of the qualities that both account for his past success and provide a pointer to his future actions. There is the honesty, the taste for the risky venture, the total focus on the job in hand, the relish for a challenge, the passion for physical activity, the desire to win, the acute observation, even under stress, the concern for others, the compassion, the gift for articulate communication, the talent for making news which has turned him into a national icon.

"It is amazing how often Marco creates a situation in which something could go wrong – and it doesn't!" Mike McKenzie, a businessman who became first a customer, then a friend, backs this conclusion with a recollection of a small episode in their relationship. "I had invited a few important heads of industry to the Oak Room for dinner. I told Marco that we would be having a quiet drink in the bar at about 7.30 and said that I'd appreciate it if he could find the time to come over and say hello. I was sitting, with a beer, with my back to the wall behind which is the kitchen. Suddenly, a spoon sailed over my shoulder and landed, right way up, without touching my hand or the sides of the glass, in my beer. Marco, keeping his promise and saying hello!"

Of a new project envisaged by the chef/restaurateur/entre-preneur/tycoon, McKenzie declared simply, "It will work because Marco will make it work. I have never seen anyone push and stretch as Marco does. He makes people feel special, but that comes from his belief that he himself is special. He has an overwhelming degree of self-confidence."

There is also, according to another friend, customer and fishing companion, the property consultant Steven Kane, "a big hole in his life, which helps explain his problems with women and his need for success". The early death of his mother accounts for an underlying melancholy: "If he was anyone else, he would need counselling; he lives in a pressure cooker – if he didn't go fishing he would go insane." Marco, says Kane, "was the apple of his mother's eye, the golden child", and with her sudden death, "something was stolen from him". He was angry with his father because "he couldn't become a mother". Marco, his friend says, "is a Malteser: hard on the outside, soft on the inside. He can be rude and insensitive – but unbelievably generous; he is very competitive, but also excruciatingly funny, with a very fast wit."

Like McKenzie, Kane has total confidence in the future of Marco the businessman and empire-builder. "I know he is a very good chef because thankfully I can afford to eat in his restaurants, but he has a natural talent for absorbing new business concepts rapidly – and adding to them. He has an incredibly quick and able mind, and it isn't loaded with preconceptions and traditional ways of thinking. He plays three-dimensional chess. Marco will not go from A to B to C – he'll go straight to E. He has a natural sense of strategy – he loves to talk about generals and their achievements."

The military image found a curious echo in the press. A dispatch from the faithful camp-follower Emily Green in the *Independent on Sunday* reported: "Marco Pierre White has started sounding like a general. He is, he says, 'building forces in London to advance into the provinces'."

Lynn Barber, writing in the *Independent on Sunday*, chose the field of fashion rather than the field of battle for her explanation of Marco's branding strategy: "Marco learned that brilliant cooking was not enough. He learned about marketing the brand name – becoming the Gucci or Chanel of the restaurant world. The game now is about maintaining standards, maintaining consistency."

Matthew Fort of the *Guardian* was not so sure of the master's sure touch. Taking the City restaurant MPW (now Big Chef) as his exemplar, he imagined it as "a template for MPWs rolled out nationwide". This would be "no bad thing for Abersock, Aberdeen or Abbots Langley, but it will be a wonder if they will be able to duplicate the level of competence at the stove of the original. Still, it is always going to be better than Kentucky Fried Chicken, Little Chef or Café Rouge, isn't it?"

Rising above such low ground, Lucy Humphries of *Square Meal* takes a flying leap into Christianity, no less. "Think of the Apostles. And that's the thing about Marco and his teams. They come, they learn, they stay and then they're released back into the wild to spread the word." The results are apparent, she claims, all over London and increasingly in the provinces. "This messianic approach is not to be confused with Terence Conran, who has had a similarly exhilarating effect on our dining habits. Marco believes you can take good food to the masses … but, for him, Conran sells design, not food. 'He's the best retailer in the business,' he says, with genuine admiration but no desire to emulate."

Indeed, Marco was proving to be no mean designer and retailer himself, even in the Conran heartland of Soho: he had, according to Humphries, turned "the magnificent dining room in the Regent Palace Hotel", which had been "frequented by naff coach parties and tourists in polyester slacks", into "an essential destination for those who simultaneously want good food, style and a fashionable buzz".

What, though, does the great retailer and designer think of his increasingly visible rival? Speaking in expansive mood in his newly opened, dashingly designed rooftop restaurant, Le Coq d'Argent in the City, Sir Terence is gracious:

> I admire Marco, I enjoy his company, but I think he is in danger of turning from an artist into a commercial artist, like Andy Warhol with his art factory. He is undoubtedly a Jekyll and Hyde: so many good qualities, so many ridiculous – "what a genius I am" and all that. He has done an awful lot of good for the restaurant business, but the chef now is more important than the restaurant and is becoming a media person, who is not behind the stove – not even supervising the chefs who are cooking. I fear for him, busy developing his empire when his real talent will be wasted. I met him in the Oak Room not long ago and he sat down with me for two hours at the busiest time – so he wasn't cooking.

(One is tempted to respond: Do the passengers tickled pink at dining at the Captain's table for a couple of hours believe that their safety is jeopardized by the quality of the people on the bridge during that time?) "Marco and I have one thing going for us," Sir Terence concedes, in apparent contradiction to his earlier views, "that is, we can draw a team from one restaurant to open another. We can also offer career development within the organization – and we can develop our people."

Conran's view of Marco as an absentee chef would certainly be disputed by the man himself – and by those who form the general's *brigades* (to use the French term for the kitchen workforce). Although the work of a restaurant kitchen is, rightly, usually compared to a military operation in its need for order, discipline, speed, timing, fraternity, mutual respect, teamwork and the abolition of any nine-to-five mentality, the Yorkshire–Italian maestro takes a more romantic view. Talking to Bob Mullan for his book on chefs, Marco explained his work thus:

> I conduct – I'm like a conductor with a symphony, I've got to
> conduct the service. I've got to see everything that's going out. I've
> got to touch everything, I've got to feel everything, I've got to taste
> things ... so I stand on the *passe* with my two head chefs ... there's
> the stove behind you with a hotplate where the waiters stand – the
> food goes over it – left and right of me are my two key men. I'll
> either help with the fish or I'll help with the meat, depending on
> where my help is required.

All in all, the scene evoked seems closer to the real restaurant action than the drawing-board view of a Conran.

Marco's friend, collaborator and Mayfair neighbour David Coffer has been involved with the restaurant world for 33 years. He sees Marco very clearly: "Well, he's got his costume, hasn't he?" – a reference to the tailored tweed, corduroy and chef's whites described

---

fish tales

Fishing is the full stop in every week.

– Marco Pierre White

---

by the painter Jonny Yeo as "Marco's modified squire outfit". For Coffer, "the future is to build up identity – to appear now and then. If he branded his name internationally he would lose control – it would be like Chinese plate juggling. What he should say is, 'Mayfair is my domain. Feudal! Barons will come to me and pay homage. This is the menu from my castle.' Occasionally he will make a sortie, a visit." Coffer sees his friend as rising above mere cuisine to the creation and management of great hotels – "a master, like César Ritz". He also points out that Marco is not alone: "Mati is very strong, and Jimmy [Lahoud] is very, very strong – and bloody good in meetings."

Marco's partner Jimmy Lahoud, as described by Matthew Fort of the *Guardian,* "is one of those shadowy figures who have a substantial impact on the restaurant industry in London, but whose names rarely pop up in the press". Fort sees Lahoud – scion of a prominent family of Lebanese Maronite Christians, with a degree in food technology from Cairo University – as the antithesis of Marco. "He is small, dapper and quick, the essential urban man." The relationship runs deep, and has done so ever since 1986, when the young Marco turned up at the door of Lahoud's restaurant, Leoni's Quo Vadis, in search of work.

Marco says of Lahoud, "He's a good man, is Jimmy. His strengths complement my weaknesses." Though firmly based on friendship, there is an extremely pragmatic side to the relationship. "What Jimmy brings to the party," according to Marco, "is that he checks the gross profit on the food every single week. He checks the GP on the wine, the bar stocks. He checks the wages. It means I've got someone guarding my back constantly." As Lahoud sums it up, "I say to Marco, 'You see to getting the public in, I'll see about making the money.'"

The arrangement seems ideal. Marco generates the publicity, gets the critics in, presents the public profile, devises the menus, develops the recipes, finds and trains the cooking staff – and lends his name as the guarantee of quality. Jimmy reads the accounts, checks the deals, minds the details, keeps an eye on the margins and, in the words of Matthew Fort, "makes sure that no one is ripping his partner off".

Whatever the nature of the relationship, Marco, according to Fort, has a clear business objective: to launch the company, MPW-Criterion, on the stock market in two or three years' time. This is the next logical step in what Fort calls "the process of the chef-as-product", citing Alexis Soyer from the 19th century, Marcel Boulestin pre-war and Anton Mosimann today as precursors.

If the notion of a stock market flotation – which would be likely to value the group at £30 million – was provided by Marco, it is the direct opposite of the one he gave to another journalist, Lynn Barber: "I can't ever see myself going public. People might talk about it – it seems the fashionable thing to do. But once you go public, you're dealing with accountants and they tell you how many flowers you can have. I can't imagine being told how to run my company. I'm an entrepreneur, not a corporate man."

This stance, in turn, might come as a surprise to an unreconstructed corporate man such as his other partner, Charles Allen of Granada, even if the latter's enlightened view is that "I do think we are compatible because I feel that we have both challenged the received wisdom of our particular industries". That, at least, is demonstrably true in the unique case of Marco Pierre White.

For Jimmy Lahoud (talking to Lynn Barber), "Marco's still the same bright, sparkling, naughty, Machiavellian character. He plays games, he's still young, constantly bubbling. But he used to be much more emotional, hyperactive and temperamental. Now he's subtle, mature, clever, he thinks before he speaks, he doesn't press the point by shouting and screaming. I think he's acquired a tremendous business ability and acumen – he's wised up."

The older, wiser Marco – having first reverted to his quirky youth by snatching Lynn Barber's recorder and removing the tape – also confided in her: "In the eyes of many, I lived a very enviable life. But the reality was, I wasn't a very happy person. I think back to those

Harvey's days and it was like trouble, risk, everything followed me. But it's more exciting looking back than it was living it. It was almost hell-like then. The big difference is that I'm happy with my life and happy with my own identity and at one with myself."

Marco solo

Eschewing parties, "cheap TV award ceremonies", which he regards as the drugs of his industry, interviews, photographers and even the restaurants of his peers and rivals, Marco spends his working life in one or other of his own establishments. Most of his friends are not in the restaurant business but are businessmen, artists, photographers, writers, lawyers. As his friend David Coffer points out, "Marco doesn't go to the people, the people come to Marco" – and they know where to find him, any day, from nine in the morning to three the next morning. A father figure, he needs and enjoys mothering people. Here are a few random snapshots from his working days and nights and his rare moments of leisure.

- Mid-morning at the Mirabelle. Pre-service calm. Marco cruises behind the bar, passes an open door, glimpses a white-coated young man, about 17, leaning on a stool, polishing a glass and yawning. The peace is disturbed by a frightening bellow. "Are you tired? Tired, are you? Then go home. Go home!" To a passing *maitre d'hôtel*: "What are those stools doing there? Get them out. Put them in the storeroom. Send him home. He's *tired*." Marco sails on, to talk to the odd job man, the retired former chef at the old Mirabelle who still likes to come in every day, as he has for 40 years. The boy, his face almost as white as his jacket, appears at Marco's shoulder. Before he can speak, there is a roar: "Don't you apologize! For Christ's sake, don't apologize!" The youth starts to mumble, revealing a foreign accent, about a late night, and is cut short. Marco, interested, asks, "Where are you from?" "Romania." Marco contemplates this for a long moment, then puts his hand on the boy's shoulder. "We expect better things from your country," he says gravely. "Get back to work."

- The cramped, small, stifling office of the Mirabelle, Friday mid-afternoon. Marco has clearly had a tough day. For him, there is only one solution to his problems: to go fishing. Unfortunately, all his kit is at home in Hampshire. He calls his regular suppliers in Battersea and orders a complete set of equipment – "my usual stuff". He instructs Mr Ishii, his personal assistant, to proceed to Lillywhite's on Piccadilly and buy a casual top and trousers, large size (the green Wellington boots, giant size, are, as always, behind the door). He telephones his driver in Belgravia. Staff look in at the doorway and quickly, wordlessly, leave. The fishing kit arrives and is closely examined as the delivery-man leaves, £20 richer. Takanori Ishii returns, with clothes. They are not suitable, and he is sent away again. Finally, the huge chef emerges, incongruously disguised in a navy-blue Reebok track suit, on to the busy pavement of Curzon Street, the small Japanese struggling gamely beside him with the fishing material. The Land Rover is nowhere in sight: not good news. When it arrives and the driver, Bernard Lawson, starts to say a few placating words about the traffic, he is stopped by a shout: "Don't talk to me! Just don't bloody talk to me!" As Marco is about to clamber into the vehicle, he turns to the author, who has been present throughout the scene, and, calmly and with the utmost solicitude, says, "We'll be going by your place. Can we give you a lift?"

- The Mirabelle office, lunch service just beginning. As the maestro is offering a glass of champagne to a visitor, his eye strays to one of the closed-circuit TV screens that display the activity in each part of the restaurant. He sees one of his *maitres d'hôtel* jesting with a waiter. He excuses himself, picks up the telephone and says, "Ask Mr X to come and see me." When the man arrives, Marco says, "This is the second time in a week I have seen you fooling around in front of the clients. If you have a joke to share, do it somewhere private. The client must be respected. I want you to leave service now, and go down to the pub, and buy yourself a beer – and sit down and think about your life."

- Under a footbridge on the River Avon, Marco spots a shadow in the water. "That's a very nice fish," he says eagerly to his companion, a journalist from *The Times*. "An impressive fish. It'll go like a bat out of hell." An angler already positioned on the opposite bank clearly takes a dim view of the newcomer's growing interest. Marco is unabashed. He wants the salmon. He has lost one already. The journalist recalls reports of the chef's taste for ejecting his clients. Would the rival angler suffer a similar fate? Instead, Marco cajoles him into joining forces. Soon Marco is casting away and his new friend is lying on the bridge, giving directions: "Left a bit. Right a bit. A little deeper. Perfect." On this stretch of the river, only six salmon have been caught all summer, two of them by Marco. Today he adds two more to the total.

- Staying at a country hotel in the middle of a golf-course, Marco is strolling on its perimeter with a painter friend, having asked permission to do so. They are confronted by a man who asks somewhat officiously what they are doing there. "May I ask who you are?" asks Marco. "My name is Andrew Smith," the man replies. Marco considers this information gravely, looks down from his great height and innocently asks, "Is that hyphenated?"

- The daughter of Bob Barnes, the Leeds greenkeeper on whose lawns Marco used to trespass as a boy, collecting golf balls, telephones Marco to say that she is in town with a friend, and could they meet? He has not seen her since she was his protegée at Fir Trees Primary. "Come to dinner," Marco says, and when the two arrive at the Mirabelle he seats them with two other friends who happen to be dining: the singer and actress Bette Midler, and Lord Charles Spencer Churchill, younger brother of the Duke of Marlborough.

- Looking in at the Grill Room of the Café Royal to see how things are going at a function organized by MPW, Marco spots a once-familiar face: Michael Caine, whom he has not met since the dramatic rupture of their partnership at The Canteen. Feeling that it is his responsibility, as the younger man, to make the move, Marco approaches Caine, who says, "If I'd known you were going to be here, I wouldn't have come!" Marco replies, "If I'd known *you* were coming, *I* wouldn't have come!" The two men smile wryly, shake hands and agree to meet soon for lunch.

- A young, fresh-faced customer, leaving after dinner, approaches Marco and thanks him for the fine meal he has enjoyed. Courteously employing the established formula, Marco says, "Thank you, I'll let the kitchen know," and moves on. The young man was that week's celebrity, Leonardo DiCaprio. "I didn't recognize him," says Marco later, in wonderment.

The thoughts of Chairman Marco

To mark an important anniversary, Mati gave Marco a key-ring. It was engraved with a white star and the legend "21 years at the stove". In that period he was the 16-year-old rebelliously shelling peas in the kitchens of the St George Hotel in Harrogate, the goggle-eyed apprentice in the wonderland of the Box Tree in Ilkley, the manic genius of Harvey's in Wandsworth, the tempestuous litigant of The Canteen in Chelsea, the single-minded young master chef of The Restaurant in Knightsbridge, the father burdened with the still-unresolved grief for his lost mother. All are now subsumed in this millionaire head of an organization of 400 people, already responsible for seven thriving London restaurants and, with his powerful associates, Granada, planning many more, in the capital and throughout the land, including in his birthplace, Leeds. Here, garnered on the run, is a sampler of the powerful leader's current thinking on the people and events of a peopled and eventful life:

- I am, if you like, a representation of the future. I now have the finest restaurant group in the world. Granada and I dominate London and now I want to change the face of gastronomy in Britain.

- At the Oak Room, if we break even each week we are happy. If we make a profit, it is a bonus, and we regard it as a by-product of our generosity.

- Fifty per cent of the top restaurants in Britain either are owned by me, were set up by me or are staffed by people who learned their craft under my tutelage.

- Cooking is a way of life. When I get up in the morning, I don't go to work; I just carry on with my way of life.

- I don't go out in public. I'm either cooking or fishing.

- I'm not addicted to fishing. I just miss it a lot when I haven't done it for a while.

- I do kill a lot of things. But it's all about culling. I'm a conservationist. I love nature. And I love eating!

- At work, I used to play an attacking game. Now I play a defensive game.

- My entire business strategy is based on *The Godfather*. I run my life like a Mafia don. What I saw in that film was a man who joined forces with others and built a big company to suppress his insecurity. And that is exactly what I have done. The whole structure is founded on my insecurity. I was 21 when I saw that movie, and after it I made the conscious decision that no one would ever again treat me as a second-class citizen. That was me in that film: I gave people too much respect.

- Do I ever feel vengeful? No, although Machiavelli said, "If you can't make friends with your enemies, kill them." My enemies are people who let me down, so I pushed them out of my life.

Walked away from them. I don't fall out with people – I walk away
from them.

- A liar continues to lie. He has no options.

- I have about 15 pairs of Marks & Spencer trainer bottoms that I
  wear for work. They allow you to bend down and move around.
  The old-fashioned blue check chef's trousers were not comfortable
  and you couldn't bend over in them.

- Harvey's never made any money. I sold my share for £17,500 at the
  end – but I got my freedom back. It made my name and my
  reputation. After seven years it was time to move on. I didn't see
  any future with Nigel Platts-Martin. He didn't bring anything to
  the party: he wasn't a restaurateur. Besides, I met Michael Caine – I
  was impressed, as any young man would be – and through him,
  Rocco [Forte]. That changed my life.

- Rocco is a good man. A gentleman. I have a lot of time for him, a
  lot of respect.

- Interesting, doing a restaurant so far out [in Wandsworth]. Amazing
  to think that in 1991–2 the average bill was £120 a head. I learned
  the power of PR and the influence of Michelin there. It was
  Michelin that did it for us: that rapid elevation from one to two
  stars. I wasn't commercially minded. I ran it like the two "boys" ran
  the Box Tree. Seven cooks in the kitchen, including me. Their
  values, their taste. They weren't commercially minded. Nor was I.
  Roux was commercially minded. Steak 200 grams, lamb kidneys
  150 grams a portion. Mechanical, not emotional. The Box Tree was
  emotional.

- Albert Roux was the first man ever to win three stars in Britain. The
  Roger Bannister of cuisine! Broke a fantastic record. Classical

dishes, like the lobster, the lemon tart. An exceptional man. When I was young I thought that Albert was a clever man. Older, I realize he wasn't clever. And he was arrogant.

- The boys at the Box Tree were my greatest influence. Pierre Koffmann – I like his philosophy, I just don't like his technique. I admire [Raymond] Blanc's technique, but he is inconsistent. His cuisine is designed for one man, not a team. The great three-star restaurants don't break down. Like a football team: there are eleven players, you can pass from one to the other. Raymond is a three-star chef, but he can't deliver down the line, he can't create a three-star restaurant.

- I regard myself as an old-fashioned restaurateur; I put money back into the whole dining experience, because I care about it in a way I don't think many chefs do.

- When you walk into a restaurant, the first thing you are aware of is the environment. Every detail is important. I think that foodies who say they are only interested in what is on the plate must lead pretty boring lives. I believe that when people go out to eat, they want to drink fine wine, and enjoy being surrounded by art and good company.

- Somebody told me that when you walk into a restaurant, you are the audience, and when you sit down you are the actor; I think that's true.

- The days of gastronomy are dying. People – the young – who go out two or three times a week want a good meal in nice surroundings at a fair price. They don't want the formality of great restaurants.

- I didn't try to invent gastronomy – you can't re-invent the wheel.

It's all about refinement, refining what's there. I mean, tomatoes go with basil. Chicken with tarragon. Fish and chips. Cheese and onions. I like tradition: roast chicken, *oeufs à la neige* ...

- Nature makes the great culinary combinations. We chefs are not that clever.

- Exceptional man, Terence [Conran]. It took a non-restaurateur to take restaurants and show what could be done with them!

- I haven't really changed much over the years – things have changed around me. But the people who are around me have been around me for years. In fact, I'm going back to the way I was as a child. I had my own little group – older people, like Mr Duncan [the golf pro] and the greenkeeper. The instinct to survive took over after the death of my mother. (Funny, I have no memory of my father before my mother died.) There was no time for learning, for making friends. I spent time by myself, constantly thinking. I was so strong as a child – no one could beat me. There were two boys at school from broken homes, but I was the only one whose mother had died. A teacher at my primary school – now the headmistress – wrote to me the other day, and I spoke to her on the telephone. "It was very obvious you were highly intelligent," she said. "No one could teach you anything." What she remembered was "the way you looked at people, the way you penetrated them". "Do you remember pulling my hair?" I asked. "I do," she said.

- One of the greatest things you can give a child is an education in the conventional manner. If a child can't read the questions ... I could never understand why they made me stand up and read a chapter from a book. They couldn't put me down by beating me, so they humiliated me that way. I never had a credit card until I was 30 years old. I hated filling in forms – they were like exams, they reminded me too much of my schooldays.

- My mother was the type of person who would check the chimney before putting a fire on, to make sure a bird hadn't fallen in.

- Anyone who tries to damage my family, or take away security from my family, I will fight to the bitter end.

- I don't like the idea of sending my boys away [to school]. I like to wake up with my children, go to bed with them. I don't want them to grow up too quickly. My childhood was wonderful – freedom! When I went shooting, fishing, rabbiting, I had confidence, but in the real world, so-called, I had none. Then I discovered that, with food in my hands, I could express myself. In that first kitchen, they pushed things my way, I was so enthusiastic.

- I've been compared to Jean Cocteau, which is very flattering. Like Cocteau, I pretend to be decadent, while being very disciplined.

- Self-control is true power.

- [Prime Minister] Blair is a weak man. His hair is all over the place. He's a mess. He isn't in control.

- I've got a house in the country, on this island in the river. I'll probably keep it for a while – let it go next year. It restricts me in where I go to fish – there's no excitement anymore; when you're surrounded by water, it's not the same! Early morning is the best time to go fishing – four o'clock, then back to London to work at nine. When it's on your doorstep, it loses its magic.

- All I've done is get on with my life.

• • •

Marco has been many things, and there are clearly more to come. "I have re-invented myself," he recently declared. "I have become a painter." The walls of a refurbished Quo Vadis, the Soho restaurant where he first met his partner Jimmy Lahoud, are now adorned with the art of Marco Pierre White. The controversial works of Damien Hirst have been returned to their owner, or withdrawn by him – each artist vehemently, and publicly, presenting his own version of events.

In a further complication, Hirst declared that the neophyte painter had aped his work, while Marco, citing numerous witnesses, including Hirst himself, accused his former schoolmate of blatantly copying one of his artifacts. Scenting the possibility, always alluring, of litigation, Marco threatened a writ, demanding a written apology for wilful plagiarism. While the row continued, with Hirst's mother attempting to intercede on her son's behalf, the Godfatherly Marco was sure of the outcome: "At the end of the day, he will pay his price … I know who'll win."

As for the new works, they were taken seriously enough by the (restaurant) critics. A A Gill of the *Sunday Times*, himself a painter and graduate of the Royal College of Art, and a fellow gun, allowed that Marco's paintings were better than his shooting. ("He caught me on a bad day," Marco explains.) The *Evening Standard*'s Fay Maschler was coolly and wittily impressed: "His [Marco's] own paintings and assemblages, which newly decorate the historic Dean Street premises, might persuade Damien to eat his heart out – which would be an interesting, apt step forward in the area of conceptual art."

Meanwhile, the newly self-created artist, as a long-time self-declared classicist, might well be pondering, like many of those who have followed his remarkable career, on the English meaning of the renovated restaurant's name: "Whither goest thou," Marco?

hot from the press – and the kitchen

In a calculated *coup de théâtre*, which cynics saw as a cunning pre-emptive strike but which others, like the sagacious Egon Ronay, had long foretold, Marco Pierre White informed the nation's press that he was abandoning his *métier* of master chef, quitting the stove, putting aside for ever the tall *toque* (which he had never worn) of his calling, and handing back his hard-earned Michelin stars.

"Tempestuous three-star chef gets out of the kitchen," headlined *The Times,* over a half page. "Marco Pierre White to put cooking on the back burner," cried the London *Evening Standard*. More cautiously, and over two pages, the *Daily Telegraph* qualified its headline, "Not the retiring type", with a subhead that claimed that the former chef's "powerful ambition now reaches far beyond the kitchen".

Thus 21 years in the kitchen came to a close. "My love for restaurants will never die," Marco said. "I have achieved the ultimate of three Michelin stars, but it is much more exciting chasing the stars than defending them. I want to spend more time with my family and focus my working energy on becoming the best restaurateur in the country." And not, it would seem, only in this country: there were teasing mentions, perhaps wisely taken with a pinch of *gros sel* as coming from one who has never travelled further south or west than Bournemouth, of forays into Paris and New York.

The cynics who crowed about pre-emption had their reasons, but were themselves neatly pre-empted. "I don't want Michelin saying standards have fallen and taking away my stars," Marco said, as he, in effect, handed in his stripes. But there was another, deeper reason for his decision, not conveyed to the press. "I'm the same age now as my mother was when she died, and that made me think. I'd achieved everything I set out to achieve. I'd lived a complete life over those 38 years. It was time to start again, to change direction."

marco – master chef

With astonishing prescience and impressive self-awareness, while cooking at his first restaurant, Harvey's, the young Marco Pierre White declared: "I'm just at the beginning of my career: you're not going to see the true Marco until I'm 35 or 40." At the age of 38 – and, as a Michelin-accoladed three-star chef, at the peak of his powers and the summit of his calling – he abruptly announced his retirement from the kitchen. He had, he felt, nothing more to prove.

What had he learned and – for he is the acknowledged mentor of a whole generation of talented tyros in the trade – what did he teach during those brief, hectic years? Somewhat discouragingly, his mantra has always been, "There's nothing really new in cooking – you can't re-invent the wheel." True, no doubt, but you can, as Marco recognizes, borrow, embellish, improve on the classics.

For example, the famous crème brûlée with slivers of Granny Smith (recipe on page 206) was – as far as we know – the inspiration of the great chef Guy Savoy in his Paris restaurant, from where it was translated by a young trainee in the kitchen, one Gordon Ramsay, to his restaurant Aubergine in London, where it was spotted by his former master, the ever-observant and duly appreciative Marco Pierre White. "Nobody ever invented a new dish: you'd have to invent new ingredients first."

He had learned about such practices in his first employment, at the remarkable Box Tree in Ilkley, where he acquired the foundation of his knowledge from the restaurant's two English owners, who were entirely without training in the classical French cuisine. Their method was to visit all the two- and three-star restaurants of France, to eat, taste, remember and then, back in Yorkshire, to recreate and refine. "If people would only spend more time tasting what they are cooking instead of worrying about germs, the quality of their cooking would soar."

It was this knowledge, enriched by his experience with the French masters practising their art in London, that he took to his own first restaurant. "It's enlightening to look back at some of my earlier menus at Harvey's; there are some very simple combinations there, classics, which I obviously relied on while I was perfecting my craft."

This *simplicity* was something Marco continued to pursue in subsequent locations, in the teeth, as it were, of opposition from his own clientele. Even as he became the youngest chef ever, anywhere (including France), to achieve three stars, at The Restaurant in the Hyde Park Hotel, he was regretting that "in France, because of the different food ethic or culture, the great chefs can get away with offering a simple roast chicken, grilled sea bream with a red wine sauce or salmon with a sorrel sauce. That cutting through to the essentials is something I'd like to do as well, but nine out of ten of my customers wouldn't understand it."

"Classical" did not mean only *haute cuisine*. While Marco was happily being "profligate with truffles and caviar" at The Restaurant, he was also, while maintaining the highest standards, bringing his art down to a more affordable level at The Canteen. Dishes perfected there are to be found, often prepared by the same chefs, at his subsequent establishments, like the Criterion and the Titanic. The Mirabelle strikes the middle note: luxury at acceptable prices. In any of them, the simple classics – a chunk of succulent cod, mashed potatoes, lemon tart – are likely to feature on the menu, cooked to the same consistently high standard.

Marco, the master chef become restaurateur, continues to believe that the foundation of all good cooking lies in the classical marriages (of which he is fond of citing fish and chips). "But you must use your brain to rethink them, make them relevant, give them a contemporary beauty." While acknowledging that "no domestic cook can ever achieve what we can, because they lack the hands, the time, the facilities, the finance", he believes that any of his recipes, because of their intrinsic simplicity, can be successfully interpreted in the home – *enjoyably*.

A final word: "Be generous. Be extravagant. Without generosity there is no love, and without love there is no understanding."

PUBLISHER'S NOTE

For readers who would like to pursue further their interest in the recipes of Marco Pierre White, the following books are available: *White Heat* (1990), *Wild Food from Land and Sea* (1994), *Canteen Cuisine* (1995), and *The Mirabelle Cookbook* (1999).

Harvey's

Salad of marinated sea scallop

Serves 2

2 large scallops

1 tablespoon olive oil

6 coriander seeds, crushed

salt, black pepper, sea salt

6 pieces salad de mâche (on the stalk but trimmed)

3 tablespoons olive oil and 1 tablespoon white wine vinegar mixed for vinaigrette

6 baby spinach leaves

8 small centre leaves of oakleaf lettuce

4 thin slices raw beetroot

4 long thin slices carrot

2 chicory leaves, diced very finely

4 coriander leaves, finely julienned

chervil, to garnish

1   Thinly slice the scallops and place neatly on the inner edge of two large plates. Coat them sparingly with olive oil. Sprinkle on the crushed coriander seeds and a little freshly ground black pepper. Place in the fridge for 10 minutes.

2   Mix the leaves, season and add a little vinaigrette, and arrange neatly in the centre of the plates to form a salad 7.5 cm (3 in) high. Season the vegetables and chicory, add a little vinaigrette, and carefully place on the salad. Finish with a piece of chervil and the julienned coriander.

3   Season the scallops with a little sea salt.

Fresh fillet of sea bass velouté with caviar

Serves 2

3 tablespoons olive oil
salt and freshly ground black pepper
1.3 kg (3 lb) wild sea bass, scaled, filleted and pinboned
16 pieces mangetout
100 g (4 oz) white radish
juice of ½ lemon
30 g (1¼ oz) oscietta caviar
chervil to garnish

For the velouté
6 shallots, thinly sliced
15 g (½ oz) unsalted butter
500 ml (18 fl oz) white wine
500 ml (18 fl oz) Noilly Prat
1 litre (1¾ pints) fish stock
1 litre (1¾ pints) double cream

1   To make the velouté, cook the shallots in the butter until
    softened, without colouring. Deglaze with the wine and Noilly
    Prat, and boil to reduce to a syrup. Add the fish stock and boil
    to reduce by half. Add the cream, bring to the boil and simmer
    for 5 minutes to reduce to a coating consistency. Pass through a
    fine sieve. If not using immediately, cover with cling film and
    chill.
2   Lay out a piece of cling film 20 cm (8 in) square, and smear
    with a little olive oil, salt and pepper. Place one sea bass fillet

skin down on the cling film, and season the top and brush with oil. Then wrap neatly in the cling film, creating a vacuum. Repeat with the second fillet. Preheat a fish steamer large enough to take both parcels.

3   Trim the ends of the mangetout and cut into thin strips. Skin the radish and cut into similarly sized julienne.

4   Place the sea bass parcels in the steamer and cook for 6 to 8 minutes.

5   Blanch the vegetable julienne in salted water until croquant (crunchy) – about 1 minute. Drain well, place in a bowl, season and add a little olive oil. Keep hot.

6   Heat the velouté in a pan to simmering point. Remove the fish from the steamer and take off the cling film. Smear a few drops of lemon juice and of olive oil over both sides of the fish.

7   To serve, place the vegetables evenly on each plate, with the fish on top, skin side up. Take the velouté off the heat and add the caviar. Pour the sauce all around each plate, and garnish with chervil.

Tarte au chocolat

For the pâté sucré
750 g (1 lb 10 oz) unsalted butter
220 g (8½ oz) icing sugar
6 egg yolks
60 ml (2 fl oz) water
750 g (1 lb 10 oz) flour

For the filling
4 eggs
3 egg yolks
175 g (6 oz) sugar
250 g (9 oz) unsalted butter
375 g (13 oz) dark chocolate

1 To make the pâté sucré (sweet pastry), cream together the butter and sugar, and add the egg yolks and a drop of water. Then slowly mix in the flour, stirring and kneading, and gradually adding the rest of the water, until you have a smooth pastry. Chill for at least an hour.

2 Preheat the oven to 180°C/350°F/Gas 4. Take 300 g (10 oz) of the pâté sucré (the rest can be kept in the freezer until needed), roll out to 3 mm (⅛ in) and use to line a tart ring measuring 25 cm (10 in) in diameter and 2.5 cm (1 in) deep. Blind bake in the oven until brown.

3 To make the filling, whisk the eggs and egg yolks with the sugar for about 5 to 10 minutes in the blender, to make a sabayon. Melt the butter and chocolate gently in a bain-marie, and allow to cool. Then fold the chocolate butter through the sabayon until fully mixed.

4 Pour the filling into the blind-baked pastry case, and replace in the oven for another 10 minutes to bake. Allow to cool before serving.

The Titanic

Caesar salad

Serves 4

4 heads Baby Gem lettuce
100 g (4 oz) croûtons cooked in garlic olive oil
8 marinated anchovy fillets
8 long parmesan shavings

For the Caesar dressing
3 cloves garlic, crushed
50 g (2 oz) parmesan finely grated
6 salted anchovy fillets
1 teaspoon wholegrain Dijon mustard
1 egg yolk
3 tablespoons white wine vinegar
120 ml (4 fl oz) olive oil
1 dash Worcestershire sauce
salt
freshly ground black pepper

1   To make the dressing, blend the crushed garlic, grated parmesan
    and anchovy fillets into a fine paste, add the mustard and egg
    yolk, and whisk. Pour in the vinegar, and whisk in the olive oil.
    When emulsified, add the Worcestershire sauce and seasoning to
    taste.
2   Wash and break up the lettuces into leaves, dry them, and mix
    in the dressing. Distribute between four bowls. Place the garlic
    croûtons around the outside of each bowl, and two anchovy
    fillets and two shavings of parmesan on top.

Cod à la Kiev

Serves 2

2 cloves garlic
1 bunch flat leaf parsley, chopped
zest of ½ lemon
80 g (3¼ oz) unsalted butter, softened
1 kg (2 lb 3 oz) cod, scaled and filleted, giving two 180 g (7 oz) fillets
50 g (2 oz) seasoned flour
2 eggs, beaten
150 g (5 oz) fine breadcrumbs
sunflower oil for deep frying
1 lemon, halved, to garnish
2 small bunches watercress, to garnish

1   Crush the garlic to a fine paste, then add the chopped parsley, lemon zest and soft butter, and mix well. Place in a piping bag.
2   With a sharp filleting knife, cut a small slit under the skin of each fillet, then pipe the garlic butter into the fish, being careful not to overfill.
3   Dip the cod fillets first in seasoned flour, then in the beaten eggs, and finally in the breadcrumbs.
4   Preheat the sunflower oil to 160ºC/320ºF/Gas 2½, and deep fry the cod until crisp and golden. Serve with pommes frites, and garnish each plate with half a lemon and a bunch of watercress.

Sherry trifle

Serves 6

18 discs of 5 mm (¼ in) sponge, 6 of them 2 cm (¾ in) and 12 of them
    3 cm (1¼ in) in diameter
1 tin pear halves, diced into 5 mm (¼ in) squares
1 tin peach halves, diced into 5 mm (¼ in) squares
a few roasted nuts and fresh raspberries, to decorate

For the jelly
½ bottle medium sweet sherry
150 ml (5 fl oz) water
150 g (5 oz) caster sugar
4 leaves gelatine, soaked

For the custard
12 egg yolks
200 g (8 oz) caster sugar
500 ml (18 fl oz) milk
1 tablespoon Bird's Custard Powder

For the crème chantilly
500 ml (18 fl oz) double cream
100 g (4 oz) caster sugar
few drops vanilla essence

1   To make the jelly, mix the sherry, water and sugar in a pan and
    bring to the boil. Add the gelatine, and then allow to cool.
2   To make the custard, combine the egg yolks and sugar. Bring the
    milk to boiling point, and pour over the egg yolk mixture. Cook
    over a very low heat (no more than 80ºC/180ºF), stirring
    continuously using a wooden spoon. Add the custard powder
    and whisk until slightly thickened. Allow to cool.

3 Place a small disc of sponge in the bottom of each of 6 cocktail glasses, with a spoonful of the pears and peaches on top. Pour on some of the jelly, and place in the fridge to set. Repeat this process until the glasses are filled up to within 2.5 cm (1 in) of the top.

4 Place a large sponge disc on the top of each. Spoon on a layer of custard.

5 To make the crème chantilly, whip the cream and sugar until it reaches ribbon consistency, and stir in the vanilla essence. Pipe the crème chantilly on top of each trifle, and decorate with a few raspberries and roasted nuts.

The Criterion

Spring rolls with crab

Serves 4

300 g (10 oz) white crab meat
2 red peppers
1 bunch spring onions
sesame oil
75 g (3 oz) root ginger
soy sauce
freshly ground white pepper
12 sheets filo pastry
100 ml (3½ fl oz) clarified butter
1 lemon
vegetable oil for deep frying

For the mayonnaise
1 egg yolk
300 ml (10 fl oz) vegetable oil
1 teaspoon Dijon mustard
juice of 1 lemon
1 teaspoon white wine vinegar
salt
pinch cayenne pepper

1   Make a mayonnaise using the egg yolk, gradually whisking in
    the vegetable oil until thick. Add the mustard, lemon juice,
    vinegar, salt and cayenne pepper to taste.
2   Heat the deep fryer to 180°C/350°F. Clean the crab meat,
    checking for pieces of shell.

3   Place the red peppers under a hot grill until the skin blisters, being careful not to burn the flesh. Peel and cut into a brunoise (small dice).

4   Top and tail the spring onions. Cut half of them into fine julienne and the other half finely on the bias. Sweat the latter in a little sesame oil until soft, then drain.

5   Cut the root ginger into fine julienne, blanche in boiling water and refresh, then dry on kitchen paper.

6   Combine the crab, ginger and cooked spring onion, adding just enough of the mayonnaise to bind. Season with a little soy sauce and pepper.

7   Take the first filo sheet, fold in half and brush with a little clarified butter. Place some crab mixture on the sheet, leaving 2.5 cm (1 in) at the bottom and both sides. Fold in the sides over the mixture, then the bottom edge. Roll tightly. Repeat with the other 11 filo sheets and the remaining crab mixture.

8   Mix two parts of sesame oil to one of soy sauce, and stir in the red pepper brunoise. Arrange in a circle on each of four plates. Dress the julienne of spring onion with a little lemon juice and seasoning, and place in the centre of the plates.

9   Fry the spring rolls in the vegetable oil until golden brown, drain on kitchen paper and season. Place three in the middle of each plate, with the remaining spring onion on top.

Fresh salmon, pomme sautée with truffle-infused cabbage cream

Serves 4

500 ml (18 fl oz) chicken stock
200 g (7 oz) smoked pork belly
3 large outer leaves of Savoy cabbage
4 large baking potatoes
goose fat
300 ml (10 fl oz) double cream
truffle oil
salt and freshly ground black pepper
four 150 g (5 oz) slices from a side of salmon, filleted but with the skin on
seasonal salad leaves

1   Heat the chicken stock and pork belly in a pan. Bring to the boil, then remove from the heat and allow to infuse. The pork can be left in the stock when cold.
2   Wash the cabbage leaves, and cook them in boiling salted water until completely soft. Refresh in iced water, strain off and liquidize until they make a purée.
3   Cook the baking potatoes whole in boiling salted water for about 20 minutes until two-thirds cooked. Remove from heat and allow to cool. Then cut each potato into five slices, and gently sauté in the goose fat until golden brown.
4   Place the pork and chicken stock back on the heat, add double cream, and bring to the boil. Add the cabbage purée and a little truffle oil, season and remove from the heat. Sauté the salmon, skin side down first, until pink.
5   Place the sautée potatoes on the plate with the cooked salmon on top. Add the seasonal salad leaves on top of the salmon, and pour the sauce around the sautée potatoes.

Crème brûlée Granny Smith

Serves 4

500 g (1 lb 2 oz) egg yolks, whisked
280 g (10 oz) caster sugar
1.5 litres (2½ pints) double cream
400 ml (14 fl oz) milk
8 vanilla pods
brown or demerara sugar
a little Granny Smith apple juice

For the apple chips
4 Granny Smith apples
50ml (2 fl oz) lemon stock syrup

1 Preheat the oven to 100ºC/210ºF. Mix the whisked egg yolks
   and sugar together. Bring the cream, milk and vanilla pods to
   the boil in a pan, and pour over the egg yolk and sugar mixture.
2 Pour the crème into four 5 cm (2 in) foil cups; place in a bain-
   marie in the oven for about 30 minutes. Refrigerate overnight.
3 Sprinkle brown or demerara sugar on top of the crèmes, and
   caramelize under a hot grill. Allow to cool briefly, then run a
   knife around each foil cup, turn out on your hand, and place on
   a plate (with the caramel on top). Place 6 or 8 apple chips into
   the sides, and pour a little apple juice around them.

To make the apple chips
1 Cut each Granny Smith apple in half, core the halves and slice
   thinly.
2 Brush each slice lightly on both sides with a lemon stock syrup,
   place them on parchment paper and leave to dry.
3 Place them in the oven at 100ºC/210ºF briefly before serving.

The Mirabelle

Smoked salmon properly garnished

Serves 4

500 g (1 lb 2 oz) sliced smoked salmon
freshly ground black pepper
50 g (2 oz) shallots, finely chopped
20 g (¾ oz) flat leaf parsley, cut into thin strips
50 g (2 oz) baby capers
50 g (2 oz) gherkins, chopped
2 hard-boiled eggs, grated
2 lemons, halved, and wrapped in muslin
slices of buttered brown bread, to serve

For the horseradish cream
100 g (4 oz) horseradish sauce
2 tablespoons double cream
cayenne pepper
juice of ½ lemon

1 Divide the salmon equally between 4 plates. Grind a little black pepper over them.
2 Place the shallots, parsley, capers, gherkins and egg in five separate piles on the edge of the smoked salmon, and put the lemon halves, wrapped in muslin, in the middle.
3 To make the horseradish cream, mix together the horseradish sauce, cream, cayenne and lemon juice. Serve it in a little jug on the side, with the buttered brown bread.

Roast pheasant properly garnished

Serves 4

8 slices streaky and 4 slices back bacon
two 1.1 kg (2¾ lb) dressed pheasants
6 sprigs of thyme
12 juniper berries
salt and freshly ground white pepper
goose fat, for roasting

For the gravy
1 celery stick, 1 onion and 1 carrot, all chopped
2 cloves garlic, peeled and halved
100 ml (3½ fl oz) white wine
sprigs of thyme
200 ml (7 fl oz) veal stock

For the bread sauce
400 ml (14 fl oz) milk
1 slice onion
1 clove
4 slices white bread, diced
salt and white pepper

For the chips
4 large Maris Piper potatoes
vegetable oil, for deep frying

1   Preheat the oven to 200°C/400°F/Gas 6. Arrange 4 slices of
    streaky bacon across each pheasant, and into each bird put 3
    sprigs of thyme and 6 juniper berries. Season them inside and
    out, then tie and truss them.
2   Heat the goose fat in a roasting tin on top of the stove, then seal

the pheasants on all sides. Roast in the oven for 25–30 minutes. Remove and allow to rest in a warm place.

3 Grill or pan-fry the back bacon, and keep warm.

4 To serve, remove the pheasants' legs, trim the feet, and make a cut between the thigh and the drumstick. Remove the breasts, and slice each into three. Place the slices of breast on top of a thigh and a drumstick. Serve the bacon, bread sauce, gravy and game chips separately. Popular accompaniments are Brussels sprouts, braised cabbage or roast parsnips.

To make the gravy

1 Place the cut celery, onion, carrot and garlic in the tin in which the pheasants were cooked, and roast them till golden.

2 Add the wine, thyme and a little salt and pepper, and boil until the liquid has virtually evaporated. Add the veal stock, and any juices that have come off the pheasants. Bring to the boil and simmer for 3 minutes. Pass through a sieve into a gravy boat.

To make the bread sauce

1 Bring the milk to the boil with the onion and clove, and simmer for 2 minutes. Strain out the onion and clove.

2 Add the bread to half the milk, mash together and season. Cover with cling film, and keep warm.

To make the chips

1 Peel the potatoes and slice on a mandolin. Wash the slices in hot water, then drain and dry them well in kitchen paper.

2 In very hot oil, deep fry the chips until golden brown. Drain on kitchen paper, and serve.

Whisky jelly with red fruits

Serves 6

½ bottle of whisky
250 ml (9 fl oz) water
400 g (14 oz) caster sugar
7 leaves gelatine
2 punnets of raspberries
2 bananas
1 punnet of blackberries
1 punnet of blueberries

1   Place the whisky, water and sugar in a pan and bring to the boil.
2   While the whisky mixture is heating up, place the gelatine in ice-cold water. When the whisky mixture reaches boiling point, take it off the heat and add the soaked gelatine. Stir slowly. Allow to cool a little.
3   Pour a thin layer of jelly into each 150 ml (5 fl oz) pudding mould, and place in the fridge to set. Keep the rest of the jelly warm.
4   When the moulds are set, add a layer of raspberries to fill the width of the mould, upside down, and then add a little jelly without covering the raspberries. Return to the fridge.
5   When the jelly is set, cover the raspberries with more jelly and allow to set again.
6   Slice the bananas really finely, and place evenly on top of the raspberries. Cover with jelly and allow to set again. Repeat this process with the blackberries and blueberries (slicing the blackberries in half if they are too large).
7   Chill the moulds thoroughly until they are set. Turn them out and serve.

The Oak Room

Marinière of shellfish with calamari and basil

Serves 1

1 medium carrot
1 medium courgette
1 bulb fennel
½ celeriac
1 bunch basil
100 ml (3½ fl oz) olive oil
200 ml (7 fl oz) white wine
50g (2 oz) diced onion
25 g (1 oz) celery
1 sprig thyme
1 bay leaf
400 g (14 oz) mussels
400 g (14 oz) clams
2 scallops, cleaned and sliced horizontally
garlic salt
salt and freshly ground black pepper
2 baby calamaris, cleaned and cut into julienne
vegetable oil, for deep frying
juice of ½ lemon

1 Chop the carrot, courgette, fennel and celeriac into 5 mm (¼ in)
  dice.
2 Blanch the basil for 30 seconds and refresh, then purée with the
  olive oil.
3 Bring the wine to boiling point in a pan with the diced onion,
  celery, thyme and bay leaf, and cook the mussels and clams in it

for 2 minutes. Remove the mussels and clams from their shells, and keep warm. Retain the cooking liquor.

4   Poach the sliced scallops briefly in some of the cooking liquor.

5   Bring the remaining cooking liquor to the boil, add the diced carrot, courgette, fennel and celeriac, and cook for 10 seconds. Season with garlic salt, salt and pepper. Whisk in the purée of basil and olive oil. Do not boil again.

6   Fry the calamari julienne in a deep-fat fryer until crisp, then sprinkle with salt and lemon juice.

7   To serve, mix the mussels and clams together and place on the plate. Pour over a little of the cooking liquor. Place the fried calamaris and the scallops on top.

Ballotine of salmon with herbs

Serves about 14

1 salmon weighing 3.5–4.5 kg (8–10 lb), skinned and filleted
salt and freshly ground white pepper
cayenne pepper
2 bunches each chervil, chives, tarragon, dill and flat parsley, finely
    chopped
1½ leaves bronze-leaf gelatine
225 g (8½ oz) fromage blanc with herbs (see below)
25 g (1 oz) keta salmon eggs
chervil sprigs

For the fromage blanc with herbs
250 g (9 oz) fromage blanc
50 g (2 oz) shallots
15 g (½ oz) garlic
handful of chives
250 ml (9 fl oz) double cream

1 Season the salmon fillets on both sides with salt, pepper and
   cayenne, and leave for 15 minutes. Dry with kitchen paper.
2 Lay out two sheets of cling film, one third overlapping, so that it
   will extend about 2.5 cm (1 in) beyond the salmon. Lay another
   two sheets on top of them in exactly the same way, to produce a
   double layer.
3 Place half the chopped herbs on top of the cling film, and press
   the skin side of one of the salmon fillets on to the herbs. Place
   the gelatine leaves on top of the salmon. Now lay the other
   salmon fillet "head to tail" on top of the first, skin side up, and
   coat with the remaining herbs.
4 Roll up the cling film tightly lengthways to form a sausage
   shape, excluding as much air as possible, and tie both ends. Tie

the salmon at three equal intervals, to maintain its shape. Then roll in a wet tea towel and tie in the same way. Weigh the salmon.

5   To cook, poach in enough heavily seasoned water to cover, at 65°C/150°F, for 3 minutes per 450 g (1 lb). Leave in the liquor to cool for 1 hour, then remove. Cool completely, then refrigerate for 24 hours.

6   To serve, remove the cloth and cling film, and cut carefully into slices about 3 cm (1¼ in) thick using a very sharp knife. Place a slice just below the centre of each plate, with a quenelle of fromage blanc and a little mound of keta. Garnish with chervil.

To make the fromage blanc with herbs

1   Place the fromage blanc in a piece of muslin, tie securely with string and suspend over a bowl for 24 hours so that every drop of liquid drips out.

2   Chop the shallots, garlic and chives very finely, and fold them into the fromage blanc.

3   Whip the double cream to soft peaks, and fold it into the fromage blanc mixture. Refrigerate until required. (This makes more than you will need for the ballotine of salmon.)

Grilled lobster with herbs and garlic, béarnaise mousseline

Serves 1

3 litres (5 pints) fish stock
1 live lobster
250 g (9 oz) unsalted butter, softened
1½ teaspoons chopped garlic
2 tablespoons finely chopped parsley
salt
béarnaise mousseline sauce, to serve

1   Bring the fish stock to the boil, blanch the lobster in it for 4 minutes at 75ºC/170ºF, then leave to rest in a warm place for 5 minutes.
2   Into the butter, mix the chopped garlic and parsley and some salt. Preheat the oven to 200°C/400°F/Gas 6.
3   Cut the lobster in half lengthways, remove the flesh from the claws, clean out the head, and remove the flesh from the body. Fill the shell with some of the garlic butter. Return the flesh to the shell, and cover with the rest of the garlic butter. Cook in the oven for about 4 minutes.
4   Serve with a béarnaise mousseline sauce on the side.

Pigeon from Brest with foie gras, pomme purée and fumée of cêpes

Serves 2

1 pigeon
200 g (7 oz) foie gras
4 large Savoy cabbage leaves
freshly ground black pepper
caul fat (crépinette)
clarified butter, to fry
salt and cushed black peppercorns
pomme purée, to serve

1 Remove the breasts from the pigeon, keeping the winglets attached, skin them and trim off any fat or sinew. Cut the winglets off at the second knuckle, and clean well.
2 Cut the foie gras into two equal pieces, and leave at room temperature to soften.
3 Blanch the cabbage leaves in well-salted boiling water for 2–3 minutes until soft.
4 Place the softened foie gras on each pigeon breast, wrap tightly in cling film, and mould in your hands to form the same shape as the pigeon breast. Refrigerate until hard.
5 Season the top of the foie gras with pepper only, then wrap each breast in two blanched cabbage leaves.
6 Lay out the caul fat/crépinette on a smooth surface, and place the pigeon at one edge. Carefully wrap the pigeon, making sure the cabbage is the same shape as the breast and foie gras. Trim off any excess crépinette.
7 Steam the pigeon for 12 minutes over a medium heat, then finish by frying gently in clarified butter.
8 Sprinkle each breast with salt and crushed pepper, cover the knuckle with a small cutlet frill, and serve with potato purée.

Crème caramel Box Tree, friandise

Serves 6

500 ml (18 fl oz) milk
4 eggs
1 egg yolk
1 teaspoon vanilla extract
300 g (10 oz) caster sugar
100 ml (3½ fl oz) water
60 ml (2 fl oz) cold water
12 raisins

1   Place the milk in a pan and bring to a temperature of
    80ºC/176ºF. Whisk together the eggs, egg yolk, vanilla extract
    and 100 g (3½ oz) of the sugar, and pour on the hot milk. Pass
    through a fine sieve.
2   Cook the remaining sugar and the water until it reaches a dark
    caramel, then add the cold water to stop the cooking.
3   Place a spoonful of caramel and 2 raisins into each of 6 small
    dariole moulds. Place the moulds in a deep tray filled with hot
    water. Fill the moulds with custard, and cook at 130ºC/250ºF
    for 35 minutes until just set. Refrigerate.

Caramelized pineapple with vanilla and spice, glace fromage blanc

Serves 2

1 vanilla pod, chopped into 5 cm (2 in) pieces
1 large pineapple
300 g (10 oz) caster sugar
2 vanilla pods, chopped into small pieces
1 red chilli, chopped
50 g (2 oz) root ginger, chopped
2 bananas, chopped
50 ml (2 fl oz) dark rum
200 ml (7 fl oz) water
fromage blanc ice cream, to serve

1   Dry the 5 cm (2 in) vanilla pieces in the oven at 90°C/200°F overnight.
2   Peel and core the pineapple, and stud with the dried vanilla pieces.
3   Place the sugar and small vanilla pieces in a large pan and cook to a dark caramel. Stir in the chilli, ginger and banana. Turn off the heat, and add the rum and water. Leave to infuse for 24 hours.
4   Preheat the oven to 170°C/325ºF/Gas 3. Strain the sauce through a fine sieve. Place the pineapple and sauce in a large ovenproof pan and cook for 1½ hours, basting every 10 minutes until the pineapple is caramelized. Serve with fromage blanc ice cream.

Index